Effects of climate change on the profitability of carbon credit sales

A case study on *Tectona grandis* plantations located on the Pacific Coast of Costa Rica

Nina Becker

The correspondent thesis for the degree of Master of Science in International Development Studies at Wageningen University and Research Centre was accomplished in July 2009 with supervision of:

Rolf Groeneveld (Supervisor)
Environmental Economics and Natural Resources Group
Wageningen University and Research Centre, The Netherlands

Victor H. Meza (Co-supervisor)
Instituto de Investigación y Servicios Forestales
Universidad Nacional, Costa Rica

Nina Becker

EFFECTS OF CLIMATE CHANGE ON THE PROFITABILITY OF CARBON CREDIT SALES

A case study on *Tectona grandis* plantations located on the Pacific Coast of Costa Rica

ibidem-Verlag
Stuttgart

Bibliografische Information der Deutschen Nationalbibliothek
Die Deutsche Nationalbibliothek verzeichnet diese Publikation in der Deutschen Nationalbibliografie; detaillierte bibliografische Daten sind im Internet über http://dnb.d-nb.de abrufbar.

Bibliographic information published by the Deutsche Nationalbibliothek
Die Deutsche Nationalbibliothek lists this publication in the Deutsche Nationalbibliografie; detailed bibliographic data are available in the Internet at http://dnb.d-nb.de.

Cover picture: Teakholzplantagen in Cabuya, Península de Nicoya, Costa Rica © Nina Becker

∞

Gedruckt auf alterungsbeständigem, säurefreien Papier
Printed on acid-free paper

ISBN-10: 3-8382-0074-8

ISBN-13: 978-3-8382-0074-3

© *ibidem*-Verlag
Stuttgart 2010

Printed in Germany

To my family

Foreword

During the time when preparations for the international negotiations for a climate agreement after Kyoto have been moving towards their culmination- the 15th Conference of the Parties (COP15) and 5th Conference of the Parties serving as the Meeting of the Parties to the Kyoto Protocol (COP/MOP5) in Copenhagen-this book was being finalized. The events of this last past year - the negotiations as such, the Copenhagen Accord as the highly discussed outcome of Copenhagen, the carbon markets hit in the aftermath, the debate around climate science, the vindication of accused climate scientists and the IPCC, the UNFCCC meetings following Copenhagen, the Oslo Forest and Climate Conference, the IUFRO World Congress and many more events on climate and forests- all together create the plot for a play on the international stage where climate change is the main character, and forests are among the lead characters. The play has more than anything reached a momentum, where the needs for scientific and practical progress on forests and climate change issues have not only become most challenging but also most promising. The international policy audience is pressing for quick and reliable recommendations to build upon during the coming climate change negotiations that the research community is struggling with (see also Seymour, 2010).

Although this book has not been among the audience, it remains a valuable contribution to the scene- in particular to the literature on forests, climate change and carbon sequestration. Its results and recommendations have the potential to provide useful insights for the research and policy community as they are moving towards the 16th Conference of the Parties in Cancún, December 2010. Having seen the considerable attention put on forests during the COP15 In Copenhagen-specifically on the inclusion of the mechanism for reduced emissions from deforestation and degradation (REDD[1]) - it remains unquestionable that forests will play a central role in the post-2012 climate regime. However, to define this role of forests, negotiators and researchers equally face great challenges. As Frances Seymore, Director General of CIFOR put it during the XXIII IUFRO World Congress, research [on REDD] has made progress upwards 'the learning curve' but needs to integrate research on forests and climate change with the one on forests and communities to provide decision makers with the information needed (Seymour, 2010).

---

[1] The Copenhagen Accord as outcome of the COP15 calls for 'immediate action' on REDD+ (see Art. 6 in United Nations, 2009). REDD+ considers not only reduced emissions from deforestation and degradation but also includes issues of conservation, sustainable forest management and the enhancement of carbon stocks in developing countries.

This book has inexplicitly taken an approach that moves along the same lines as it seeks to link forest resources, climate change and forest owners. It focuses on individual afforestation and reforestation (A/R) projects that consider carbon sales in the face of climate chance induced alterations in tree productivity. As it analyzes the profitability of forest projects in a changing climate, it can provide valuable insights into mitigation and adaptation issues concerning tree plantations. At the same time, the implications for the profitability of forest projects outlined in this book in future can be challenged by various factors. A potential new regulatory framework or changes in the carbon markets and prices can result in variations of economic benefits generated. For instance, as small- scale tree plantation owners potentially might also benefit from the REDD+ mechanism in future and access carbon markets more flexibly (see also FAO and RECOFTC, 2010), revenue streams due to carbon credits sales of forest projects as described in this book might increase or be more easily attainable. On the other hand, we have seen that the carbon markets have been hit after Copenhagen. The resulting price uncertainty, especially in the regulated carbon markets, potentially leads to higher interest rates (Blyth, 2010). As the analysis in the book shows, this can have adverse effects on the profitability of forest projects. Also, average credit prices on the voluntary markets have dropped in 2009, which in particular has been attributed to the economic recession (Hamilton et al., 2010). Afforestation and reforestation have not been among the five highest earning project types with an average price below \$8.70 per tCO_2e (ibid.). That would suggest prices below the ones used in this analysis, rendering even less profits for the forest landholders and thus resulting in even lower profitability. This emphasizes once more the necessity for clear signals from the policy community to lead to strong carbon markets and carbon prices.

At the same time this book follows the rational of the twofold exertion of influence regarding forests and climate change. It draws upon the fundamental understanding that our climate, proven with observational evidence, is changing (see also Easterling et al., 2007). During the course over the last months however, this understanding and with it climate science has been questioned to a considerable extent. Despite of this politicized debate, specific research on plant growth and climate change published this month in Science (Zhao and Running, 2010) once more provides findings for the evidence that forest resources already experience and in future will experience consequences of climate change in line with Easterling et al. (2007). At the same time, the results of Zhao and Running (2010) contribute to the controversial debate about whether the consequences will have positive or negative implications as it finds that terrestrial carbon sinks are negatively related to climate variability. As such, the research also shows one of the uncertainties and the resulting challenges which the 'forest- climate change-communities' knowledge body is confronted with. Despite these and other challenges, the international community needs to remain hopeful to achieve a promising deal that conserves the forests, mitigates climate change and provides benefits to the forest- dependent livelihoods.

Nina Becker
M.Sc. International Development Studies
Wageningen, August 2010

References

Blyth, W. (2010). Climate Policy after Copenhagen: Managing Carbon Price Risk in an Uncertain World. In: Energy, Environment and Resource Governance. The Royal Institute of International Affairs: London (United Kingdom).

Easterling, W. E., P. K. Aggarwal, P. Batima, K. M. Brander, L. Erda, S. M. Howden, A. Kirilenko, J. Morton, J.-F. Soussana, J. Schmidhuber and F. N. Tubiello (2007). "Food, fibre and forest products." In: Climate Change 2007: Impacts, Adaptation and Vulnerability. Contribution of Working Group II to the Fourth Assessment Report of the Intergovernmental Panel on Climate Change. Eds. Parry, M. L., O. F. Canziani, J. P. Palutikof, P. J. Van der Linden and C. E. Hanson. Cambridge University Press. Cambridge (UK).

FAO and RECOFTC (2010). Forests and climate change after Copenhagen- An Asia-Pacific perspective. RECOFTC: Bangkok (Thailand).

Hamilton, K., M. Sjardin, M. Peters-Stanley and T. Marcello (2010). Building Bridges: State of the Voluntary Carbon Markets 2010. Ecosystem Marketplace & Bloomberg New Energy Finance.

Seymour, F. (2010). Forests, Climate Change, and Communities: Making progress up the learning curve. CIFOR: Keynote address delivered to the August 24, 2010 Plenary Session. XXIII IUFRO World Congress: Seoul (Korea). Available at: http://www.cifor.cgiar.org/publications/iufro/25TranscriptofFrancesSeymourSpeech.pdf (Accessed on: 28-08-2010).

United Nations (2009). Draft decision -/CP.15. Proposal by the President- Copenhagen Accord, (FCCC/CP/2009/L.7). Available at: http://unfccc.int/resource/docs/2009/cop15/eng/l07.pdf (Accessed on: 28-08-2010).

Zho, M. and S.W. Running (2010). Drought-Induced Reduction in Global Terrestrial Net Primary Production from 2000 Through 2009', Science, 329 (5994): 940-943.

Abstract

Forests play a fundamental role in mitigating climate change as they absorb carbon dioxide from the atmosphere and store it in biomass, soil and in timber products. Carbon sequestration and its storage constitute an ecosystem service that can generate benefits through Payment for Environmental/Ecosystem Services (PES) or carbon credits. In turn, climate change affects forest resources in terms of productivity, growth and forest distribution. Moreover, changes in productivity translate into changes in timber production, and carbon sequestration potential which may have effects on the profitability of forestry projects that consider carbon sequestration benefits in the form of carbon credits next to conventional timber benefits. To investigate these effects of climate change on the profitability of carbon credit sales, this research uses the method of an integrated assessment using the example of *Tectona grandis* plantations on the Pacific Coast in Costa Rica. For this purpose, a simple climate- yield model that serves to estimate total tree volume based on age, precipitation and temperature is calibrated with multiple regression methods. With the help of this model, future volume scenarios for timber volume and carbon sequestration potential can be estimated by applying different climate change scenarios. The resulting volume estimations are applied in the analysis to examine the profitability based on the criterion of the Joint Land Expectation Value (LEV_J) for timber and carbon sequestration benefits with discounted cash flow methods. The results of the research suggest: (1) Climate change that negatively affects tree productivity in the future will result in a decline in the overall profitability of forest projects. (2) The inclusion of carbon sequestration revenues increases the profitability of forest projects in general. (3) Carbon credits are not high enough to counteract the adverse effects of climate change on tree volume and, (4) Climate change affects regions to different extents depending on prevailing climate conditions in the areas and the respective future climate projections.

Keywords: mitigation, climate change effects, profitability of carbon credit sales, *Tectona grandis*, Costa Rica, integrated assessment, climate- yield model, Joint Land Expectation Value

Resumen

Los bosques en general juegan un papel fundamental en la mitigación del cambio climático, ya que absorben dióxido de carbono desde la atmósfera y lo almacenan en su biomasa, el suelo y en productos derivados de la madera. El secuestro de carbono y su almacenamiento constituye un servicio del ecosistema que puede generar beneficios al ser introducido en esquemas de Pagos por Servicios Ambientales/ Ecosistemas (PSA/PSE) o Créditos de Carbono. Por otra parte, el cambio climático afecta a los recursos forestales en términos de productividad, crecimiento y distribución del bosque. Además, los cambios en la productividad devienen en cambios en la producción de madera comercial, y en el potencial del secuestro de carbono, lo que puede afectar la rentabilidad de los proyectos forestales que tienen en cuenta estos beneficios del bosque. Para investigar los efectos del cambio climático sobre la rentabilidad de las ventas de créditos de carbono, el presente estudio aplica el método de evaluación integrada en plantaciones de *Tectona grandis* en la Vertiente del Pacifico de Costa Rica. Para dicho propósito se usó un 'climate- yield model', calibrado por métodos de regresión múltiple, que sirve para estimar el volumen total del árbol basado en edad, precipitación y temperatura. Con este modelo, se puede estimar el volumen total en diferentes escenarios de cambio climático que se utilizan para la calculación del volumen de madera comercial y del potencial del secuestro de carbono. Estos estimativos están aplicados en el análisis para examinar la rentabilidad basada en el criterio del Valor Esperado de la Tierra Conjunta (VET_c) con métodos del flujo de caja descontada. Los resultados del estudio sugieren: (1) El cambio climático, que afecta de forma negativa la productividad futura de los árboles, resulta en un descenso de la rentabilidad de los proyectos forestales. (2) La inclusión de ingresos por el secuestro de carbono aumenta la rentabilidad de tales proyectos en general. (3) Los créditos de carbono no son suficientemente altos para contrarrestar el efecto adverso del cambio climático en el volumen del árbol y, (4) El cambio climático afecta a las regiones en diferentes niveles dependiendo de las condiciones climáticas preponderantes en cada región y las respectivas proyecciones climáticas futuras.

Palabras claves: mitigación, efectos del cambio climático, rentabilidad de créditos de carbono, *Tectona grandis*, Costa Rica, asesoramiento integrado, modelo de clima y rendimiento, Valor Esperado de la Tierra Conjunta

Acknowledgements

With the accomplishment of this thesis, I want to take the opportunity to express my gratitude to all the people and institutions whose support has been vital in allowing me to complete this work.

First and foremost, I offer my sincerest gratitude to my supervisor Rolf Groeneveld at WUR and my co-supervisor Victor Meza at UNA for their guidance during this challenging process. Their support, patience and advice have been indispensable from the beginning until the completion of this thesis.

My research in Costa Rica would not have been possible without the support and advice of many people and institutes locally. I am deeply grateful for the experience I had at the INISEFOR and want to thank all its associates for their hospitality, encouragement, and technical assistance. My sincere thanks to Fernando Mora and Eladio Chaves for supporting my work and providing me access to their extensive data collections. I also want to give special thanks to the IMN for their assistance and their granted support of my research with data, in particular to José Retana for his advice and encouragement. I want to express my earnest gratitude to Max Campos for his interest in my work and encouragement. I also want to thank my friends and their families for the unconditional support they provided and for making my time in Costa Rica unforgettable.

At Wageningen University, I owe many thanks to the Environmental Economics and Natural Resources Group, in particular to Justus Wesseler for his assistance and support to improve my work, and to all other forestry experts consulted during this thesis for their ideas and help.

I wish to thank all the people in Wageningen and around the world that further enriched my work in many ways. Special thanks to Richard Klein for his encouragement and valuable advice during the entire process. My friends; I want to thank you for all the motivating words, the advices, the challenging discussions, the comments on my thesis, and for all the help in accomplishing to finish this work. Thank you for all the necessary coffee breaks, the delicious dinners together, and all other unforgettable experiences during this time in Wageningen. Thank you for your faith in me and your friendship. Thank you to all of you: my friends at home, Tine, Sandra, Markus, Moni, Lena, and Christoph; my housemates, Florien, Rik, Jouke and Michalis; the 'thesis support group and friends', Steve, Nicco, Markus, Odi, Hannes, Danuta, Caro, Martha, Liz, Marije, Fedes,

Joost, Ana, Hermes, Anna, Wiebke, Jean Carlo, Natalia, Tom, Nacho and Charlotte; and all my friends widespread in the world; Alina, María Angélica, Jhamna, Luis, Meli, Caro, Véro, Maria, Takis, Pavlína, Yves, Belen, and Sabina.

My last words are for the people I will be always grateful to for their love and their faith in me- my family. Thank you for your unconditional moral support, your patience and your encouragement during my studies and especially during the challenging time of this thesis.

Table of Contents

List of tables

List of figures

Abbreviations and acronyms

AIJ	Activities Implemented Jointly
A/R	Afforestation/ Reforestation
BBCR	Banco Central de Costa Rica (Central Bank of Costa Rica)
BEF	Biomass Expansion Factor
CACN	Centro Agrícola Cantonal de Nandayure (Agricultural Centre of Nandayure canton)
CATIE	Tropical Agricultural Center for Research and Education
CDM	Clean Development Mechanism
CIFOR	Center for International Forestry Research
COP	Conference of the Parties
COP/MOP	Conference of the Parties serving as the Meeting of the Parties to the Kyoto Protocol
CO_2e	Carbon Dioxide Equivalent
CS	Carbon sequestration
CTOs	Certified Tradable Offsets
DBH	Diameter at Breast Height
EU ETS	European Union Emission Trading Scheme
FAO	United Nations Organization for Food and Agriculture
FONAFIFO	Fondo Nacional de Financiamiento Forestal (National Forestry Financing Fund)
FSC	Forest Stewardship Council
GHG	Greenhouse Gas
IFAM	Instituto de Fomento y Asesoría Municipal (Institute for Municipal Promotion and Consultation)
IIED	International Institute for Environment and Development
IISD	International Institute for Sustainable Development

IMN	Instituto Meteorológico Nacional (National Institute of Meterology)
INEC	Instituto Nacional de Estadística y Censos (National Institute of Statistics and Census)
INISEFOR	Instituto de Investigación y Servicios Forestales (Institute of Forestry Research and Services)
IPCC	Intergovernmental Panel on Climate Change
IRR	Internal Rate of Return
IUFRO	International Union of Forest Research Organizations
JI	Joint implementation
LEV_J	Joint Land Expectation Value
LULUCF	Land-use, Land-use Change and Forestry
MARR	Minimum Acceptable Rate of Return
MINAE	Ministerio de Ambiente y Energía (Ministry of Energy and Environment)
MMD	Multi Model Data
NPP	Net Primary Production
NPV	Net Present Value
OLS	Ordinary Least Squares
ONF	Oficina Nacional Forestal (National Office of Forestry)
PPM	Permanent Plot Method
PNDF	Plan Nacional del Desarrollo Forestal
PRECIS	Providing Regional Climates for Impacts Studies
PES	Payment for Environmental/ Ecosystem Services
PSA	Pago de los Servicios Ambientales (Environmental Services Payments Program- ESPP)
RECOFTC	The Center for People and Forests
StA	Stem Analysis

SINAC	Sistema Nacional de Áreas de Conservación de Costa Rica (National System of Conservation Areas in Costa Rica)
SIREFOR	Sistema de Información de los Recursos Forestales de Costa Rica (Information System of Forest Resources in Costa Rica)
tCERs	Temporary Certified Emission Reductions
UNA	Universidad Nacional Costa Rica (National University of Costa Rica)
UNDP	United Nations Development Program
UNFCCC	United Nations Framework Convention on Climate Change
VPSs	Volume Production Scenarios
VS	Volume Scenarios
WD	Wood Density

1 Introduction

The Intergovernmental Panel on Climate Change (IPCC) states that climate change has an impact on forest resources (Easterling et al., 2007). Climate change in the short term but specifically in the medium and long-term might possibly impact these resources as forests are part of the terrestrial ecosystem and thus are directly and indirectly linked to atmospheric processes. The direct impact on the forest resources results from the changes in the composition and level of Greenhouse Gases (GHGs) as forests function as carbon sinks in the carbon cycle. Increased GHG levels and their altered composition can have impacts on forest growth, productivity and distribution. The indirect impact on growth, productivity and distribution however is caused by climate variability, changes in temperature and precipitation, and the frequency and intensity of extreme events that alter biogeochemical and physiological processes. Both the direct and indirect impact might lead to changes in the potential of forests as carbon sinks.

The potential of forests to act as carbon sinks is the focus of current mitigation practices that are considered to be a cost- effective strategy to combat climate change. The main mitigation practices- afforestation and reforestation- that are included under the Clean Development Mechanism (CDM) of the Kyoto Protocol- have received great attention from the policy side for their cost- effectiveness. So far, research in the field of forests and carbon sequestration has laid emphasis on determining the mitigation potential of forests, the costs and revenues of carbon sequestration, and the possibility to improve these potentials, for example through management practices. In recent years, the notion of carbon forestry projects as cost- effective mitigation strategy has only begun to change. It has been replaced by an adapted viewpoint that mitigation and adaptation strategies need to be linked. This was also made explicit during the 14th meeting of the Conferences of the Parties (COP) to the United Nations Framework Convention on Climate Change (UNFCCC) in Poznan in December 2008 by stating that forests were the central issue for a 'shared vision' to be developed (IISD, 2008).[2] Within

---

[2] Upon completion of this research, the latest Conference of the Parties to the United Nations Framework Convention on Climate Change (UNFCCC) was COP 14 in Poznań, Poland. Emphasizing forests' fundamental role in mitigating of and adapting to climate change since then has been high on the agenda in the international climate debate. For an update on the development of this debate and its implications for this research, see also the foreword of this book.

the linkages of mitigation and adaptation, carbon forestry projects are able to pursue wider objectives than solely focusing on the efficiency in absorbing and storing GHGs. Carbon forestry projects need to be acknowledged as being embedded in a wider reality (see e.g. Verchot et al., 2005; Rita et al., 2007; Yin et al., 2007; Cacho et al., 2008). This reality comprehends not only the mitigation potential of such projects but also concepts of community based management, sustainable management, biodiversity, and poverty reduction. Viewing carbon forestry projects together with these concepts highlights the possible additional benefits that these projects can provide. For instance, income generation as one of the additional benefits can contribute further to poverty alleviation, community development and sustainable development. Furthermore, interlinked solutions to adverse effects of climate change that consider these concepts help to provide goods and services necessary for forest dependent livelihoods and for combating climate change. Therefore, it is vital to consider these aspects amongst which additional income to forest landholders constitutes a central element. The additional income can be generated, for instance, through trading on the regulated or voluntary carbon markets of carbon offset units of a project in exchange for payments.

However, climate change with its direct and indirect impacts affects the productivity of forest resources and thus the amount of carbon sequestered. Consequently, also the economic incentives due to carbon offset sales are subject to change. As altering perspectives on carbon forestry projects can be encountered on policy levels, climate change induced realities for forest resource producers need to be assessed, and changes of carbon offset profitability analysed. Integrated assessments are needed that provide sufficient insight into how climate change can translate into changes in productivity and thus carbon sequestration potential, and its effects on the profitability of carbon credit sales. So far, such assessments are scarce.

1.1   Problem statement and purpose of the research

The likely impact of climate change on the mitigation potential of forest carbon sinks has consequences for the profitability of carbon credit sales and thus the overall profitability of forest projects. The mitigation potential can be affected as carbon stocks are changing due to, for example, changing growth and yield patterns, and expansion or contraction of inhabited areas. This in turn may affect the profitability, as the sales of carbon credits are potentially increasing or decreasing, impacting on income generation, on management and investment decisions in forest projects, and ultimately the exploitable mitigation potential of forests. This might be particularly significant in the case of fast growing species in tropical countries which have conditions that favour afforestation and reforestation.

Scientific research as in Alig et al. (2004), Sohngen et al. (2007), Reilly et al. (2007), and Boisvenue and Running (2006) suggests that forest resources experience consequences of climate change regarding tree productivity at present but that future impacts are uncertain depending on species and sites considered. Since forests act as carbon sinks, their potential to absorb and store carbon from the atmosphere may be affected by a warming climate due to impacts on tree growth and thus forest productivity. This changing potential has consequences for carbon forestry projects in place as well as projects in future. On the one hand, the mitigation potential might alter. On the other hand, income generation due to carbon credit sales might be subject to change. Policy makers but also landholders are confronted with a changing reality that needs to be integrated in decision making on both levels. The policy level needs to provide appropriate incentives whereas the landholder level needs to consider these incentives under the changing conditions. In order to contribute to decision making at both levels, extensive site and species specific research is necessary to determine the potential changes in productivity and the consequences for the profitability of carbon credit sales due to climate change.

This research will investigate the relationship between climate change and productivity, and how changes in productivity may impact the profitability of carbon credit sales. Given the defined problem and the purpose of the research, the general research question posed is: What are the effects of climate change on the profitability of carbon credit sales? This general research question is addressed by the following specific research questions:

1. What are the effects of climate change on tree productivity?

2. What is the impact of potentially changing tree productivity under climate change on the profitability of carbon credit sales?

1.2   Method

These detailed research questions will be addressed in an integrated assessment on climate change, tree productivity and profitability of carbon credit sales. Considering the complex impact of climate change on forest resources, the current investigation will focus specifically on changes in temperature and precipitation. The direct impacts of elevated GHG level, its altered composition, and other indirect impacts regarding climate variability, or an increased frequency and intensity of extreme climatic events are not subject of this study. To assess the potential effects of climate change on tree productivity, and thus to answer the first detailed research question, those climate variables that influence tree productivity primarily are determined by a climate- yield model estimated with field data. This climate- yield model in a first step estimates the tree productivity under present climate conditions and then serves in a second step to estimate tree productivity under changing climate conditions according to predicted climate change scenarios.

To determine the impact of potential changes in tree productivity under a changing climate on the profitability of carbon credit sales, and thus to answer the second detailed research question, a forest plantation profitability model is applied to calculate the Land Expectation Value of the forest land. This model considers both timber and carbon sequestration benefits as joint benefits of the private landholder. It analyses how the profitability based on these joint benefits and a defined cost structure is affected when present carbon sequestration potential might be subject to change due to altering yield with changing climate.

As such an integrated assessment makes a site and species specific research necessary, a case study is carried out on teak plantations located at the Pacific Coast of Costa Rica. *Tectona grandis L.f.* (teak) is a suitable species for the research due to its growth patterns, its timber product characteristics, and its significance in reforestation and afforestation measures in Costa Rica.

1.3   Organization and outline

Following this introduction, the 2nd chapter introduces background material for the research. The focus here will be to provide additional knowledge on climate change and forests, carbon forestry as a mitigation option, carbon markets and carbon credit revenues, as well as on teak and forestry policy in Costa Rica.

The 3rd chapter introduces the reader first with a broad overview of research on carbon sequestration in forestry based on a defined categorization of the existing literature. After that, the chapter elaborates on specific aspects across and within the categories of mitigation, carbon costs and revenues, management practices, profitability of carbon sequestration projects, and integrated assessment of these projects. It concludes with the importance of the present investigation in light of existing research.

The 4th chapter details a conceptual framework for an integrated assessment of the consequences of a changing climate on the profitability of carbon credit sales. The first part of the chapter gives an introduction to tree growth models, and the relationship between growth and climatic conditions. The second part of the chapter describes the concepts of multiple use forestry, capital budgeting, and decision criteria.

Chapter 5 describes the methodology for the present research by presenting the research area, the detailed research design on the climate- yield as well as the profitability model and their linkage. The last section of the chapter introduces the basic data on trees, and climate, as well as economic data that are required for the analysis.

The 6th Chapter describes the model calibration, including the specification of the model, and the calibration methods and results.

Chapter 7 presents the analysis and the results for the model and first addresses volume production scenarios and their respective volume scenarios for timber and carbon sequestration in future. Second, the profitability of forestry projects with differing included benefits in general, and the profitability of carbon seques-tration benefits in specific are examined. Its results are presented and proved in a concluding sensitivity analysis prior to the chapter's interim conclusions.

Chapter 8 completes this research by featuring a discussion, and finishing with the conclusions and the recommendations of the research respectively.

2 Background

Following the introduction, this chapter provides an overview of the thematic fields this thesis is embedded in. These interlinked fields relate to climate change, tree productivity, and carbon sequestration benefits. For an improved understanding, each of these fields is integrated in the following sections with the most relevant information for the present research that is divided between general information, and site and species specific information. As a result, this overview consists of information on changing climate and forests, international climate policy and carbon forestry, carbon sequestration benefits and the international carbon markets from a general perspective. These are followed by the sections on carbon projects and on Payments for Ecosystem/ Environmental Services (PES) in Costa Rica, as well as on teak plantations, timber products and carbon sequestration services that specifically refer to the case study area.

2.1 Changing climate and forests

The exertion of influence regarding forests and climate change is twofold. On the one hand, climate change affects forests but on the other hand, also forests affect climate change.

There exists sufficient evidence for a warming of the climate. According to the IPCC (2007), observations of increases in global air and global ocean temperatures, sea level rise, changes in precipitation patterns in different regions worldwide, and the frequency and intensity of extreme weather events, among others, provide this evidence. This observational evidence indicates that climate change affects natural and human environments. The acknowledged drivers of climate change are the high concentration of GHGs in the atmosphere due to the emissions caused by human activities since 1750. The IPCC (2007) states that it is very likely, i.e. with a probability over 90%, that increases in global average temperatures stem from the increase in anthropogenic GHG concentration and that global warming of the climate system of the past 50 years is caused partially by anthropogenic influence. The IPCC concludes that anthropogenic warming is likely to have influenced the observable changes in natural systems over the three last decades. This will impact ecosystems in general and within the ecosystems, forests will be affected (ibid.).

There exist direct and indirect specific effects based on anthropogenic activities that impact forests. First, changes in the composition and level of GHGs have a direct effect, since forests as part of the terrestrial ecosystem are linked to the atmosphere in the global carbon cycle. Forests function as natural carbon sinks as they absorb CO_2 and remove it from the atmosphere by capturing and storing it as carbon in biomass during photosynthetic processes (Amézquita et al., without year). An increase in carbon dioxide due to human activities might affect tree growth positively (Alig et al., 2004); depending on the joint impact with other factors such as changing temperature and precipitation. Second, and at the same time that GHG levels and compositions directly affect forest resources, there is an indirect effect of climate change on forests. Other factors than the composition or the level of GHGs will alter biogeochemical and physiological processes. By this, they will indirectly affect forest growth, yield and distribution. Among these factors are climate variability, changes in temperature and precipitation, and the frequency and intensity of extreme climate events. In turn, these effects in productivity and distribution might alter the potential of forests as carbon sinks (Chambers and Silver, 2004).

As forests are impacted by climate change as described above, they can also contribute to increased GHG levels and by this to climate change. In that sense, the exertion of influence is inverted. Naturally, emissions occur due to respiration at night, during the decomposition of organic matter as well as in case of forest fires. In general, these natural processes are balanced and no major increases in GHG levels can be expected. However also human activities related to deforestation, land use changes and burning of wood can significantly contribute to the global CO_2 emissions and thus to climate change (Cannell, 1996; Amézquita et al., without year). This emphasizes the vital role that forests play as carbon sinks and how they potentially can foster climate change. This is how the rationale arises for promoting forest carbon sequestration projects including afforestation, reforestation, and avoided deforestation.

For the present research, the focus is on the impact of climate change on forest resources. For this direction of influence, recent scientific evidence only suggests that forest resources already experience and in future will experience the consequences of climate change (Alig et al., 2004; Sohngen et al., 2007). Results however are not coherent on how climate change will affect forest resources regarding the different forest and species types. Boisvenue and Running (2006) state that there is a possibility that climate change will have a positive impact on natural forest productivity, without water as limiting variable, after examining data from literature of over 55 years. Also Reilly et al. (2007) find that the combined effect of climate and CO_2 mainly has positive consequences on forest productivity for most parts of the world. However, Boisvenue and Running (2006), as well as Fearnside (2004) state that too many controversies still exist of how climate change affects tropical forest biomass or to biomass related productivity. Therefore conclusions regarding the behaviour of forests as carbon sinks in the future are uncertain.

2.2 International climate policy and carbon forestry as mitigation option

Forests are the largest carbon pools of the terrestrial ecosystem. Great mitigation potential is attributed to tropical and temperate forests as they are highly productive forest types in the short and long run (Mohamed et al., 2004). This potential has led to the application of a great number of mitigation practices and the general viewpoint on these practices as being cost- effective mitigation options to combat climate change. Current forest mitigation practices include, among others, afforestation and reforestation, harvested wood product management, and tree species improvement for increasing biomass and consequently carbon sequestration (IPCC, 2007).

Until now, policy makers have embraced afforestation and reforestation activities and included them under the Clean Development Mechanism (CDM) of the Kyoto Protocol that entered into force in 2005. This mechanism allows Annex I countries, i.e. developed countries and economies in transition, to meet their emission targets based on 1990 levels with emission reduction projects in developing countries when the projects are eligible and fulfil the requirement of additionality (United Nations, 1998a). At present, the only activities related to land-use, land-use change and forestry (LULUCF) that are eligible under the CDM mechanism in the first commitment period from 2008 until 2012 are afforestation and reforestation activities occurring since 1990 (United Nations, 2006a). Afforestation in that sense is the conversion of land that has not been forested for the last 50 years by human intervention and reforestation the conversion of land of non forested land into forested land based due to human intervention that has not had forests on the 31 December 1989 (ibid.).

However, the current notion in international climate policy in general to view projects from a mitigation only perspective is being abandoned. Instead, mitigation and adaptation measures are increasingly interlinked. This also applies for forests and climate change as the emphasis is being switched away from the cost- effective mitigation potential of afforestation and reforestation towards improvements of sustainable forest management, conservation and increase of carbon stocks regarding forestry projects (UNFCCC, without year). These improvements are subject of the discussions for the second commitment period under the Kyoto Protocol. Their implementation will need to combine long term sustainable climate change strategies and sustainable development of forest ecosystems. These changing perspectives might suggest that in the future the inclusion of climate change induced realities for small plantation landholders could be taken into account. In the future, international climate policy might acknowledge and consider the potential of forest carbon projects that combine the concepts of mitigation, adaptation, sustainable management and income generation, among others. This can contribute to developing improved solutions and to refined decision making on the policy level and implementation level for future climate change challenges.

2.3 Direct and indirect carbon sequestration benefits and the international carbon markets

Carbon sequestration benefits derive from carbon credits obtained on the international carbon markets. In these markets carbon offsets are traded between governments, companies and individuals for a certain carbon price. As credits can be obtained directly through the markets or indirectly through national distribution systems, carbon sequestration benefits include both income channels. Specifically for this research, relevant carbon sequestration benefits are carbon credits as such as well as Payment for Ecosystem/ Environmental Services. Carbon credits can be directly attributed to carbon sequestration whereas PES schemes acknowledge carbon sequestration as only a part of ecosystem services (see also MINAE, 2008), and thus can only be indirectly attributed to it.

The carbon markets, on which the credits can be obtained, consist of regulatory and voluntary schemes. The CDM of the Kyoto Protocol constitutes a regulatory scheme under which afforestation and reforestation activities are eligible as mitigation practices. They are also eligible under other carbon trading mechanisms depending on their respective legislation. Regulatory schemes next to the CDM, are the Joint implementation (JI), also covered under the Kyoto Protocol regime, the European Union Emission Trading Scheme (EU ETS) and several other mandatory programmes (Taiyab, 2006; Kollmuss et al., 2008). The CDM states clearly that to achieve the emission reduction targets of the Annex I countries[3], it aims at achieving sustainable development by assisting non-Annex I countries, i.e. mostly developing countries with potential for CDM projects (United Nations, 2006b). However, the CDM market has so far been criticized for not having properly linked carbon markets and sustainable development benefits due to high transaction costs and other access barriers (Cosbey et al., 2005). In that line, voluntary markets have emerged to provide space for innovative designs in carbon offset trading (Kollmuss et al., 2008) to improve carbon offsets schemes vis-à-vis the mandated co-benefits of the CDM. Access barriers for small scale local community projects due to high transaction costs, among others, are potentially decreased in the voluntary market and thus have greater potential to contribute to benefits in form of income increases and income diversification for small landholders and local communities (Taiyab, 2005). Carbon credits of small projects such as tree plantations of private landholders or agroforestry systems can substantially contribute to increased benefits to the landholders and the environment.

---

[3] The Annex I countries committed themselves to achieve a reduction in their GHG emissions during the commitment period 2008-2012 of at least 5% with base levels in 1990. United Nations (1998b). Kyoto Protocol to the United Nations Framework Convention on Climate Change. Article 3. Available at: http://unfccc.int/resource/docs/convkp/kpeng.pdf (Accessed on: 13-09-2008).

2.4 Carbon projects and PES in Costa Rica

Costa Rica is an often cited example when it comes to host countries of carbon projects and forest conservation policies. It is also referred to as the pioneer of payment for environmental schemes[4]. For instance, Costa Rica was the first to initiate Certified Tradable Offsets (CTOs) under the Activities Implemented Jointly/ Joint Implementation (AIJ/JI) before the ratification of Kyoto (Chomitz et al., 1999). Another example to support its pioneer position is that Costa Rica has achieved a forest cover of more than 45% back in 2005 with about 23,900 km² (UNDP, 2008), after having ranked among the countries with the highest deforestation rates in the 1970s worldwide (Ortiz Malavasi and Kellenberg, without year). Furthermore, Costa Rica counts with several CDM projects that generate funds for the PES. So far, small and intermediate landholders in Costa Rica with forestland or land that can be converted into forestland are entitled to receive payments for environmental services in general by the governmental organization FONAFIFO (FONAFIFO, 2007). These payments acknowledge the important ecological and social benefits of forests and plantations due to the ecosystem goods and services they provide. These are acknowledged under the legal framework provided by the Forestry Law 7575 founded in 1996 and consider other ecosystem services that include the protection of scenic beauty, the protection of water resources and the protection of biodiversity (Sánchez, 2002).

At present, Costa Rica has six registered projects under the CDM (UNFCCC, 2009), and the latest prominent carbon sequestration project since 2006 is the COOPEA-GRI project that has been sold as an Afforestation/ Reforestation Clean Development Mechanism (A/R CDM) project to the Bio Carbon Fund for its first twelve years (FONAFIFO, 2008). Additional revenues generated by the carbon sales are said to be distributed to the farmers, and by this create a new modality of the PES scheme. However, definite designs for a new modality have not yet been made publicly available.

---

[4] The specific programme name of the payment for environmental schemes in Costa Rica is 'Pago de los Servicios Ambientales' (PSA) or its English equivalent 'Environmental Services Payments Program' (ESPP). For simplicity reasons, in the further discourse, they are referred to as PES in general.

Since the PES scheme acknowledges carbon sequestration as only part of the eco-system services, the total payment for plantations cannot be directly attributed to carbon sequestration. Since the new PES modality taking into account carbon sequestration directly is not available yet, landholders receive benefits for carbon sequestration only indirectly through the original PES. Receiving PES for carbon sequestration services entails several problems. These problems are generally related to access to benefits and the amount of benefits obtained. It is therefore arguable whether the PES for the establishment and maintenance of plantations provides sufficient additional revenue, particularly in areas with high land opportunity costs. Other problems that prevail with the PES, next to insufficient financial support, are long lasting application procedures and other access barriers that impede landholders from participating in the PES scheme (Hernández, pers. comm. a).

As a consequence, to enable landholders to take carbon sequestration benefits into account, access to sufficient financial support needs to be guaranteed. This in turn leads to an increased supply of an ecosystem service which at the same time may potentially increase the income of the landholders. Therefore it is necessary that PES schemes need to account appropriately for carbon sequestration. In addition to a design of appropriate national payment schemes, the possibility for participation in the voluntary markets needs to be exploited.

2.5 Teak plantations, timber products and carbon sequestration services

Costa Rica's forest cover experienced a decline from 1950 of 72% to nearly 24% in 1984 (MINAE and PNDF, 2002). It was only from the beginning of the 1970s that the Costa Rican reforestation strategy started to take off (Zbinden and Lee, 2005). The two most important species in the reforestation efforts are *Tectona grandis* and *Gmelina arborea* (melina). Despite the fact that melina covers about 45% of the total number of the planted trees (FONAFIFO and ONF, 2006), teak is considered of greater importance in the tropical regions because it is a high yield plantation species with a fast growth process. It is considered a valuable forest resource as it results in high quality timber, is easy to plant and has a good initial growth process (Chaves S. and Fonseca G., 2003; Pérez, 2005).

From an economic point of view, increasing worldwide demand for high quality timber and teak's fast growth processes and excellent timber properties make it an attractive investment option in the tropical regions in general (Keogh, 2002). Although tropical tree plantations cover only 1.4% of the total forest area in Costa Rica, they hold great economic value since 90% of the plantations can be used commercially (McKenzie, 2004). After banana and coffee production, forest resources from tree plantations rank third in the national economy of Costa Rica (Wo Ching Sancho, 2001). From a biological or physiological point of view, teak is attractive since it is more common, its rotation period is longer than for melina and it has a very fast growth rate at the beginning of the rotation period (Chaves S. and Fonseca G., 2003). The physiological characteristics make teak, next to its financial attractiveness due to timber sales, also important for potential carbon sequestration. Costa Rica also has particular advantageous environmental conditions for teak (Pérez, 2005) resulting in teak plantations that have developed successfully during the last decades (ONF, 2004). Although many of the 40,000 ha of teak plantations are owned by private industries (Chaves S. and Fonseca G., 2003), small and intermediate landholders benefit from teak with respect to its economic benefits and benefits from ecosystem services.

With its large dispersion in the tropics, the particular suitable environmental conditions in Costa Rica, and its potential for carbon sequestration for being a fast growing species and for producing long living wood products, teak plantations and teak timber have a substantial potential to contribute to mitigation of climate change and at the same time have co-benefits for the landholders. Cubero and Rojas (1999) support this as they find that taking into account carbon sales in addition to timber benefits can theoretically lead to an increase in the Net Present Value and the Internal Rate of Return of teak plantation projects in Costa Rica. In order to realize this potential, payment schemes and carbon market access need to be advantageous for small and intermediate landholders. In turn, mitigation potential can be maximized since incentives for improved sustainable management of the plantations that integrates carbon sequestration are provided.

3 Previous studies

The majority of the literature on the economics of carbon sequestration in forestry deals with the concept of cost- effective mitigation options to combat climate change. An early workshop on 'Economics of Carbon Sequestration in Forestry' in 1995[5] already criticized the lack of sound economic analysis of projects to mitigate climate change by forestation (Sampson and Sedjo, 1997). This has led to erroneous comparisons of mitigation options within different sectors such as the forestry or energy sector (ibid.). Therefore in the last years, a great amount of research on carbon sequestration aspects of forest projects and of other land use options has emerged to assist policy makers in defining the most appropriate climate change strategies and related policies in an increasing complex climate policy environment on the way to Post- Kyoto. Recently, the focus on forest projects as cost- effective mitigation strategies has been subject of change. The aim has been to integrate additional aspects to the cost- effectiveness criteria. Projects are evaluated, for instance, regarding their economic benefits to the landholders or to the respective country, and are evaluated in particular regarding their provided environmental benefits such as watershed quality or biodiversity. Thus, not only the carbon sequestration potential and costs are investigated, but also aspects of forest carbon sequestration with its impacts on and potentials for poverty reduction, sustainable development, community development, institutions and biodiversity. In addition, the differentiation between mitigation and adaptation within carbon sequestration forestry becomes increasingly indistinct as climate change has an impact on the forest itself. These changing aspects of research on carbon sequestration in forestry to assist the policy level are taken into account in the present research on forest carbon projects by focusing on the profitability for landholders. However, the present research problem is based on the fact that this profitability of carbon credit sales to landholders is subject to change due to consequences of a changing climate. By this, the research addresses a specific potential additional benefit of these projects within integrated ecological- economic research. As a result, the investigation integrates the concepts of income generation in the settings of adaptation as well as mitigation

---

[5] The workshop on 'Economics of Carbon Sequestration in Forestry' took place in Sweden, Bergendahl from May 15 until May 19 in 1995 and its contributions have been published in 'Critical Reviews in Environmental Science and Technology, Volume 27 (Special)'.

regarding forest carbon projects and by this goes beyond pure cost- effectiveness aspects of mitigation projects. The research is settled within various thematic fields that have been presented in chapter two with background information. Parallel to these thematic fields, the existing literature regarding carbon seques- tration projects in forestry is first categorized and second, presented in more de- tail in the sections of this chapter. Each section presents the literature on cross categorical themes that are relevant for the setting of the research. After that, the implications of the presented previous studies on the present research are sum- marized.

3.1   Categorization

Before the individual thematic fields are addressed in the next section to support the implications for the present research, the related categorization of the litera- ture is subsequently introduced. This categorization identifies the categories scale, scope, land-use options, type of approach, as well as type of assessment. Each of the categories is presented briefly with respective examples. The thematic fields that follow this overview in 3.2 are settled within and across these catego- ries but are described in greater detail due to its importance for the present re- search.

According to the scale of a forest project (local, national, regional, or global), re- search on carbon sequestration differs widely in its approaches and outcomes. Global approaches involve different vegetation types and species (Perez-Garcia et al., 1997), whereas national, regional, and local might focus only on one species or vegetation type (Solberg, 1997; Shvidenko, 2006).

Research on carbon sequestration in forestry can also be differentiated in its scope. As mentioned above, the focus of carbon sequestration in forest projects can be purely economic. In that case, only cost- effectiveness criteria are used to compare carbon potentials and costs of afforestation, reforestation and avoided deforestation projects for an effective climate change strategy. However, the scope of the research can also involve externalities of these projects and consider the spill over effects for human beings and the environment in terms of conserva- tion, development and poverty reduction. Recent studies have emerged as re- sponse and critique to the simple cost benefit approach and with the aim to integrate a broader scope. Noordwijk et al. (2008) for instance, emphasize that the land use with the greatest theoretical additional carbon value does not necessarily coincide with the greatest benefits for local livelihoods. Recent studies that address the integration of other non- timber benefits next to carbon sequestration and the contribution of forest carbon projects to poverty reduction (Sanchez, 2000; Cacho et al., 2008), sustainable development (Verchot et al., 2005; Li et al., 2006; Rita et al., 2007; Yin et al., 2007), as well as community development (Murdiyarso et al., 2005) and biodiversity (Solberg, 1997; Verchot et al., 2005), reflect the present concerns about carbon sequestration projects in a broader context.

In the literature, studies can be found for different types of land uses such as bare land, agricultural land, land for agroforestry, plantations or natural forests. For these land uses carbon sequestration and benefit potentials are estimated of current practices. Theoretical benefits with respect to carbon sequestration mitigation potential, landholder profitability or other externality effects of land use change are analysed and compared.

Studies can also be classified into those that apply either a bottom up or a top down approach. Whereas a top down approach relates to global scale of projects and mitigation objectives, the bottom up approach involves single or small projects identifying all carbon flows and benefits involved. Thus, the latter relates to the individual forest owner or individual species and studies on issues such as the impact on optimal rotation and profit from forest activities in joint production.

The type of assessment of carbon sequestration in forestry can help to differentiate the existing literature in integrated and non integrated approaches. Integrated approaches link economic models with biological, ecological or vegetation cover models and consider the future productivity of forests and its impacts on timber (Perez-Garcia et al., 1997; Sohngen and Mendelsohn, 1997; Thompson et al., 1997), and non- timber markets (Sohngen and Mendelsohn, 1997).

3.2   Thematic fields within and across categories

In the following, the thematic fields of importance for the research, within and across the above described categories, are presented in more detail. Relevant studies are grouped in these thematic fields. They contribute to the present research by first indicating the different focus of the research over time and by presenting important findings that are summarized in section 3.3. The focus of the thematic fields lies on the subsequent questions. What is the mitigation potential and the potential mitigation of forest carbon projects (section 3.2.1)? What are the true carbon costs and revenues (section 3.2.2)? How do carbon sequestration and management practices affect each other (3.2.3)? Are forest carbon projects profitable from a private point of view (3.2.4)? And the last section (section 3.2.5) addresses the question: which integrated assessments exist in the study field and what are their implications?

3.2.1 Mitigation potential, tropical forests and potential mitigation

Across the categories, research in economics of carbon sequestration in forestry relates to a reliable estimation of the carbon sequestration potential and of its related costs as well as benefits. An estimation of the carbon sequestration potential of different land uses on varying scales has been undertaken in an extensive amount of studies (Jong et al., 1995; Binkley et al., 1997; Masera et al., 1997; Parks et al., 1997; Sohngen and Mendelsohn, 1997; Swisher, 1997; Yin et al., 2007; Somarriba et al., 2008; Strengers et al., 2008). Also the quantification of carbon losses and gains of land use changes (Sanchez, 2000; Kirby and Potvin, 2007) has been prominent in order to identify the mitigation potential of different land uses in general, and of forest projects in specific. In addition, studies also compare the mitigation potential not only among alternative land uses such as agroforestry (Jong et al., 1995; Sanchez, 2000; Verchot et al., 2005; Antle et al., 2007; Rita et al., 2007; Roshetko et al., 2007; Soto-Pinto et al., 2007; Cacho et al., 2008; Somarriba et al., 2008; Takimoto et al., 2008), or plantations for biomass energy (Swisher, 1997; Hooda and Rawat, 2006), but also compare the mitigation potential of forest projects to other mitigation measures such as direct mitigation of fossil fuel emissions. According to Lin et al. (1999), afforestation measures are economically preferable over direct mitigation measures. Other comparisons are made regarding taxes or subsidy schemes for decreased atmospheric CO_2 levels (Grainger, 1997; Hoen and Solberg, 1997; Ley and Sedjo, 1997a; Ley and Sedjo, 1997b).

Considering the potential role that tropical forest, including plantations, play in the global carbon cycle, they are of great importance for mitigation as outlined for instance by Cannell (1996) and investigated during the last years by authors such as Schroeder (1992), Brown et al. (1993) or Lal (2005). These authors estimate the carbon sequestration potential in vegetation and soil in the tropics. Whereas natural forests are vital for long term carbon accumulation (Ortiz and Kanninen, 1999), forest plantations and agroforestry systems, in turn, have higher uptake rates that eventually make them more interesting for mitigation measures (Cubero and Rojas, 1999; Redondo-Brenes, 2005). That is, according to Binkley et al. (1997), even the case although plantations as carbon sequestration projects are considered to be low or negative in costs.

Studies on the potential mitigation in turn investigate the potential of forest projects to be included in the regulated carbon markets- mostly in the CDM under the Kyoto Protocol. The number of studies that examine the eligibility and additionality of tree plantations in Latin America for the CDM mechanism has increased in the past. For instance, Vliet et al. (2003) study six plantations in Brazil with the result that nearly none of them are eligible for CDM and that CDM inclusion of plantation projects should be taken with caution. Argüello et al. (2007) focus their study on teak plantations in Panama in order to determine the potential to be included in the CDM mechanism. Few only, for instance Somarriba et al. (2008), relate directly to the voluntary markets instead to the CDM markets, since these associate too high entry costs to make carbon credits profitable.

3.2.2 Carbon costs and revenues

Related to the sequestration potential, research studies aim at determining the real costs of carbon sequestration and storage (Binkley et al., 1997; Grainger, 1997; Parks et al., 1997; Plantinga, 1997; Swisher, 1997; Thompson et al., 1997; Strengers et al., 2008), or the additional benefits or costs of land use change (Shively et al., 2004; Tassone et al., 2004; Behan et al., 2006) in order to give recommendations on preferable project strategies among different forest projects or projects of other land uses. Van Kooten and Sohngen (2007), for example, show in their review on various studies regarding costs for carbon credits via forestry activities that these costs vary widely depending on the specific settings of the projects. On the overall, this impacts the cost- effectiveness of forest carbon projects and makes site specific research necessary.

In specific, Shively et al. (2004) for example estimate the incremental costs for carbon storage when cropland is transformed into agroforestry or into timber production land. Considering the benefits and costs, they conclude that agroforestry systems should be favoured for carbon storage over reforestation projects in a developing country. Also Tassone et al. (2004), but for a developed country, conclude that afforestation of agricultural land without subsidies does not seem profitable for private landholders and that the same subsidies actually decrease carbon sequestration provided. Behan et al. (2006) even state that despite afforestation funds, the incentives in developing countries are not high enough for switching from agriculture to forestry at all.

The carbon revenues commonly estimated in these studies often use prices from the participation in regulated and voluntary carbon markets or they use the amount of money that is channelled to landholders via subsidies or tax schemes. Revenues at present can be insufficient to make forest carbon projects profitable to the landholder. This can be related to high certification costs in the regulated markets (Cacho et al., 2004; Somarriba et al., 2008), or a subsidy structure that is suboptimal, for instance, because of its inappropriate link to fossil fuel taxes (Hoen and Solberg, 1997). Despite these latter impediments, it can be concluded that revenues need to be sufficiently high to make any land use project regarding carbon sequestration profitable.

3.2.3 Carbon sequestration and management practices

There exists a mutual relationship between carbon sequestration and management practices. On the one hand, management practices influence the potential of carbon stored in plantations and will consequently have impacts on benefits and costs, among others. Literature suggests that the carbon sequestration potential of plantations can be influenced by silvicultural practices according to Dixon (1997), Marland et al. (1997), Sohngen and Mendelsohn (1997), Thompson et al. (1997), and Garcia-Gonzalo et al. (2007). It also can be altered via an increase of the plantation area per se due to its attractive potential to absorb atmospheric CO_2 (Sohngen and Sedjo, 1999; Sedjo and Sohngen, 2000). On the other hand, the inclusion of carbon sequestration and its revenues also has implications for the management of plantations. In that line, Diaz-Balteiro and Rodriguez (2006) as well as Huang and Kronrad (2006) conclude that the optimal rotation period varies with the inclusion of carbon sequestration revenues. They also find that the optimal economic and the optimal carbon rotation period differ from each other when sequestration is included (Huang and Kronrad, 2001). The effect from possible increased revenues on the sequestration potential and the implications for management is also studied. The research of Stainback and Alavalapati (2002), for instance, suggests that increasing carbon revenues e.g. via subsidies or taxes, lengthens the optimal rotation period and augment the Land Expectation Value (LEV) as well as the supply of carbon sequestered. Tassone et al. (2004) find instead that only if carbon sequestration is considered the only social benefit, inclusion of carbon sequestration will lengthen the optimal rotation period whereas subsidies for afforestation would decrease the rotation period.

3.2.4 Private profitability of carbon sequestration projects

Plantation and agroforestry systems can provide additional benefits to the landholder in terms of carbon credits or payments for environmental services, among others. Studies about landholder profitability due to carbon sequestration options within carbon sequestration in forestry mainly focus on agroforestry and shifts from agriculture to the latter. Fewer studies also include plantation projects or consider them solely.

The great amount of research on agroforestry, carbon sequestration and additional income to the farmer suggests that profitability of carbon sequestration projects is a relevant issue in the current literature. In line with that, Verchot et al. (2005) consider additional income due to agroforestry, and Takimoto et al. (2008) conclude that carbon credits can possibly serve development of subsistence farmers. Furthermore, Sánchez (2000) indicate that carbon credits reduce poverty and achieve food security in Africa while they provide environmental benefits at the same time. Roshetko et al. (2007) also advocate smallholder agroforestry systems in South East Asia under CDM as they contribute to sustainable development as well as to emission reduction. The potential of agroforestry in carbon sequestration profitability is supported by other literature suggesting that agroforestry leads to more additional profits than agriculture when other environmental benefits than sequestration are considered (Rita et al., 2007). Also Antle et al. (2007) support carbon sequestration as they conclude in their study on Peruvian terrace and agroforestry practices that the potential to raise farm income increases up to 15%. Furthermore others, like Cacho et al. (2008), determine critical variables to make reforestation or agroforestry projects an appropriate land use in place for carbon credits and thus help reduce poverty. Aune et al. (2005), however, find that the inclusion of carbon payments cannot generate sufficient income when compared to the costs of small size forestry and agroforestry projects to justify all projects.

The economic profitability of plantations when including carbon sequestration only has been investigated far less than when agroforestry is considered. The majority of the cases settle on national or regional scale for one or more plantation species as shown in the research, for instance, undertaken by Cubero and Rojas (1999), Stainback and Alavalapati (2002), Gutierrez et al. (2006), Huang and Kronrad (2006), and Caldwell et al. (2007). Cubero and Rojas (1999) conclude in their study on carbon sequestration sales of three different plantation species in Costa Rica that revenues are positive but differ by species. Also Huang and Kronrad (2006) conclude that the inclusion of carbon sequestration, among other impacts, increases the profitability of loblolly pine plantations in the US based on selling carbon credits. Gutierrez et al. (2006) arrive at the same conclusions in their case study that evaluates five different plantation species and their profitability of plantation forestry projects under the CDM mechanism in Colombia. However, their research emphasizes that timber as well as certified carbon prices are affecting landholders' profitability and either revenue stream- timber or carbon- affects its counter revenue negatively which has a strong influence on the optimal forest management applied. In addition, they concluded that temporary certified emission reductions (tCERs) will be the most profitable carbon credit for carbon revenues (ibid.). Not carbon sequestration sales but subsidies and a carbon sequestration favouring tax scheme are the focus of the analysis of Stainback and Alavalapati (2002). The results of their analysis on the optimal rotation period and the LEV including non- timber benefits in a case study in the US suggest that carbon sequestration increases the LEV and thus can represent possible additional profitability to the landholders. Distributional aspects also need to be considered as Caldwell et al. (2007) emphasize in a case study on the impact of an A/R programme on income and carbon sequestration potential in China. The forest activities are stated to be profitable in the long term only when landholders can directly benefit from CO_2 credits as subsidies distributed by the government do not continue beyond a certain year and will therefore lead to long term profitability losses (Caldwell et al., 2007).

3.2.5 Integrated assessment of forest carbon projects

The assessment of the profitability of carbon sequestration under altering climate needs to link the vegetative response of forests on climate change and its subsequent impacts on smallholders and the economy as such. This makes interdisciplinary research necessary (Lindner et al., 2002a; Lindner et al., 2002b). Authors such as Perez-Garcia et al. (1997), Sohngen and Mendelsohn (1997), and Verchot et al. (2005) have addressed climate change as having impact on the vegetation within integrated impact assessments in the forest sector.

These integrated impact assessments in general can be classified as linking, coupling or integrated modelling according to Lindner et al. (2002b). For forest sector impact assessments, growth and yield models of tree species are combined in an integrated manner with forest product models (Lindner et al., 2002a; Garcia-Gonzalo et al., 2007), or timber market models (Sohngen et al., 2001). The simulation of forest growth and yield under climate change in turn is either undertaken with the help of process based models (Garcia-Gonzalo et al., 2007), or empirical models (Westfall and Amateis, 2003), or based on a combination of both models (Nuutinen et al., 2006). While Kellomäki et al. (1997) use a process based model for one species, Garcia-Gonzalo et al. (2007) address a process based ecosystem model that allows growth and yield estimations for several species. Depending on the aim of the study, the use of process based models might be preferable over empirical models. Nuutinen et al. (2006) for example, state that empirical based studies are not appropriate to simulate growth under climate change for a region.

While most of the ecological modelling under climate change focus on the alteration of temperature and precipitation, other studies in turn model the impact of elevated CO_2 on the growth of forest resources. When only changes in temperature and precipitation are analysed, Westfall and Amateis (2003) for instance, conclude that yield can be negatively affected in particular due to changes in temperature. This is also suggested by Clark et al. (2003), who find a negative effect of temperature on forest net primary production (NPP) in the tropical rainforest. However, Westfall and Amateis (2003) suggest that when next to climate variables also CO_2 is examined, growth can be positively affected, whereas Clark et al. (2003) consider the effect of CO_2 not strong enough to result in a positive impact of climate change on forest productivity. Garcia-Gonzalo et al. (2007) again find an overall increase in timber yield as well as in the carbon sequestration potentials considering temperature, precipitation and CO_2 levels. Reilly et al. (2007), in addition to the analysis of the combined effect of climate variables and increased CO_2 levels, consider tropospheric ozone in contrast to many studies in the past. According to their study, climate change and elevated CO_2 levels imply positive but small yield and production effects in most cases for forestry, whereas ozone is considered unfavourable for these effects (ibid.).

Most research on integrated ecological and economic assessment can be found on the simulation of future forest growth due to climate change and its impact on timber markets through timber yields. Only a few scholars also consider the impacts on carbon sequestration potentials or biodiversity (Sohngen and Mendelsohn, 1997; Garcia-Gonzalo et al., 2007). Other few, such as Reilly et al. (2007), study comprehensive effects on the economic sectors when forest growth and growth of other land use resources are simulated and compared.

The above mentioned research discipline that integrates timber markets under a changing climate focuses on the effects on overall timber production (Kellomäki et al., 1997; Lindner et al., 2002a; Nuutinen et al., 2006), as well as the effects on the carbon sequestration potential and the implications for management adaptation (Garcia-Gonzalo et al., 2007). Implications on the timber production vary in these studies. Whereas some studies suggests differences in whether timber production increases or decreases depending on the future climate (Lindner et al., 2002a), other studies present scenarios that all lead to increasing timber production (Nuutinen et al., 2006; Garcia-Gonzalo et al., 2007). Various studies on climate change and forest resources focus on the spatial aspect of these implied future timber production yields. Sohngen et al. (2007) or Easterling and Apps (2005) suggest that due to a changing climate it is likely that there will be important shifts in supply and demand of forest products in general. Sohngen et al. (2007) support the view that for the medium (2025-2065) and long run (after 2065) market shares for forest and timber will increase for tropical and subtropical regions in case of adaptation in boreal and temperate regions being insufficient. Easterling and Apps (2005) state that climate change and its impacts on forest productivity will have great consequences for local forest ecosystems; although being equilibrated on regional and global level. They emphasize, in line with Sohngen et al. (2007), that trends will favour producers from developing countries.

Studies also differ in the number of climate scenarios and the amount of forest management regimes applied, depending on the objective. Various climate and management regimes are integrated in the assessments of Lindner et al. (2002a), Lindner and Cramer (2002), and Garcia-Gonzalo et al. (2007) with differentiation in extreme management types ranging from economic objectives of timber production to objectives of ecosystem conservation (Lindner and Cramer , 2002) to biodiversity objectives (Garcia-Gonzalo et al., 2007). Other studies, in contrast, refer to only one regime and study the impact on the rotation due to climate change (Kellomäki et al., 1997), or analyse the impact on the optimal sustainable management scenarios (Nuutinen et al., 2006).

The differing results in timber yields and carbon sequestration potentials that can be found in literature on integrated assessments of climate change and forests productivity, support the fact that impacts are site and species specific (Lindner et al., 2002a). Also Cannell (1996) and Saxe et al. (2001) emphasize the importance of specific response of trees and forests to climate change and management which in future will link to adaptation measures by selecting site appropriate species.

3.3 Interim conclusions and implications for the current research

The implications for the current research derive from the findings of the studies in each respective thematic field. As the first two fields demonstrate, the prevailing focus has been on mitigation and cost- effectiveness and provides relevant findings to support the substantial mitigation potential of fast growing plantations in the tropics. In addition, the studies on carbon costs and revenues imply for the present study that often costs outweigh the revenues in forest carbon projects and by this make projects insufficiently profitable for the landholder. Studies on the mutual relationship of carbon sequestration and management practices highlight the possible impact of one on another. They also illustrate a deviation from the focus on mitigation potential and cost- effectiveness towards a focus that considers aspects of sustainable management. The main findings for the present research suggest that carbon sequestration augments the profitability of a forest project and can lengthen the rotation period. Studies regarding the profitability of carbon sequestration projects show that the generation of additional income is a relevant issue within carbon sequestration research. Furthermore, they indicate that carbon sequestration can but does not necessarily increase the overall profitability of forest carbon projects. The literature also shows that most research on that field is carried out on agroforestry rather than plantation forestry. Therefore the present research can be of valuable contribution to the study field.

The overall conclusion, however, derives from all fields combined with the studies presented on integrated assessment. In all the cases of research on climate change impacts and forest resources presented, even if carbon sequestration potentials are considered and carbon costs are estimated, the inclusion of carbon markets does not take place at present in integrated assessments in accordance with the cited literature. Hence, profitability impacts for the landholders are only implied due to an early investment return, but not due to the inclusion of carbon sequestration. In particular regarding plantations, there are few studies that link the vegetative response from forests and its consequences based on the impact of climate change on tropical forest productivity. Non integrated studies, which are extensive on tropical tree plantations, in turn address joint timber production and carbon sequestration with focus on the impacts on optimal rotation age and on the LEV in great terms. These studies, however, do not include that productivity and thus carbon sequestration potential might be subject to change due to climatic alterations. Therefore, further research is necessary that considers climate change, site and species specific tree productivity in the tropics and the profitability from carbon credits sales. For this purpose, an integrated forest carbon impact assessment is a suitable tool that will need to focus on the landholder level in a bottom- up approach. Current non integrated research focusing on other than profitability aspects of the integration of carbon sequestration in forest projects such as poverty reduction, community development and biodiversity impacts are vital to address in integrated assessment in future but cannot be subject of the following research.

4 Conceptual framework

The conceptual framework for an integrated assessment of climate change effects on the profitability of carbon credit sales draws upon the interaction of climate and forest productivity, as well as the profitability of non- timber goods i.e. carbon sequestration in forest project investments. The first section of this chapter on tree productivity and climate, introduces tree productivity and its explanatory factors (4.1.1) along with a description of the relationship between tree productivity and climatic factors (4.1.2). The purpose of this section is to provide the necessary concepts behind tree productivity and climate needed to construct a climate- yield model. The second section elaborates on the concepts regarding the profitability of non- timber goods i.e. carbon sequestration in forestry projects. It combines multiple use forestry with the focus on carbon revenues as non- timber benefits (4.2.1), and presents capital budgeting decision criteria (4.2.2) that lead to the concept of the Joint Land Expectation Value (4.2.3). The overall conclusions in this chapter summarize the concepts of both sections and highlight the importance for the purpose of the present research.

4.1 Tree productivity and climate

4.1.1 Tree productivity and its explanatory factors

Tree growth is a biological process over time describing the increase in size of a tree. As the increase is taking place over time, it is also referred to as cumulative growth, and generally follows a sigmoid curve as a function of age (Clutter et al., 1983). Growth and cumulative growth of trees constitute parameters of tree productivity and can be predicted with the help of growth and yield models respectively. Both models predict tree productivity, whereupon growth models utilize volume increments, and yield models use volume as parameter.

A standard model to describe the relationship of cumulative-growth and explanatory factors is based on the work of Schumacher (1939, cited in Clutter et al., 1983). His work determines the relationship of yield and age as log- reciprocal, with yield as the dependent and age as one of the independent variables (ibid.; see also Avery and Burkhart, 2002).

However, other factors than age explain tree productivity. A complex interaction of edaphic factors (physical and chemical properties of the soil), topography, climatic factors, and external influential factors, as well as human intervention determine the productivity of forest resources (Pandey, 1996; Bebarta, 1999). Edaphic factors determine, among others, the nutritional content of the soil and its texture, depth and drainage. Linked to topography, these properties impact for instance soil moisture and nutrient uptake (Pandey, 1996). Climatic factors, such as precipitation, temperature, light, and relative humidity affect forest tree growth directly through photosynthesis and respiration, and impact growth indirectly, for instance, by affecting transpiration (see also Bebarta, 1999). Together, soil, topography and climate factors create a microclimate that determines the conditions for forest tree growth and thus affects the yield of forest resources. Other external influential factors like fire and hurricanes as well as pests, diseases and natural mortality impact forest growth and yield. These factors are, except natural mortality, interrelated with climate and thus climate change (see also IPCC, 2007). Furthermore, human intervention regarding management activities such as irrigation, thinning, pruning and felling has important effects on productivity as well (see also Bebarta, 1999).

Growth and yield models can integrate these site factors in the log- reciprocal relationship of cumulative growth and age based on a common approach presented by Brack and Wood (1998). Their approach uses the Schumacher model allowing the integration of any site factor in its linear form in order to quantify the impact of site factors on productivity (ibid.).

4.1.2 Tree productivity and climatic factors

The importance that climatic factors play in affecting tree productivity provides the rationale for the work of Weck (1970) and Pandey (1996). Both estimate tree productivity in terms of growth increments with the help of climatic factors. Weck (1970) developed a climate index for the tropical regions that Pandey (1996) refined further in his work to present a theoretical framework to estimate potential yield for tropical tree species. When predicting yield for teak in India and Myanmar by means of climatic variables, the author found that precipitation, temperature and light can be considered most influencing in tree growth (ibid.).

The amount of precipitation and precipitation patterns are considered to be the most affecting factors for growth in the tropics. The seasonal and spatial distribution of precipitation is decisive for the vegetation at a specific location. In addition to the total annual sum of precipitation, these seasonal differences are relevant for vegetation growth in the tropics. Nevertheless, it is difficult to quantify the sole effect of precipitation on plants as precipitation interacts with other climate and non- climate factors in a complex way. Pandey (1996) hypothesize for the relationship of productivity and precipitation that mean annual precipitation is positively correlated with yield until a certain limit. The author's results confirm this hypothesis as they support a linear relation until a specific optimum. Furthermore, Pandey (1996) find that after that optimum, an increase in precipitation has decreasing marginal effects on yield. (ibid.)

Regarding the relationship of temperature and vegetation growth in the tropics, high temperatures do not necessarily limit growth, as it is characteristic for temperate regions, but still can lower growth. Low temperatures also do not constitute a limiting factor for growth in the tropics as temperatures are high throughout the entire year, exceeding a growth initiating threshold temperature. Instead, the daily temperature variation is influential in the tropics. Growth can be impeded due to higher transpiration processes beyond the optimum temperature. Pandey (1996) confirms that the relationship of temperature and tropical tree growth is unclear until the present. However, the author indicates that the relationship of mean maximum temperature with growth follows a similar pattern as precipitation and growth. The author concludes that temperatures beyond a certain upper limit affect growth negatively. (ibid.)

Other climatic factors next to precipitation and temperature are highly relevant for vegetation growth. Among these factors, light is the most crucial one as it constitutes the precondition for dry matter production. Thus variables such as day length, defined as the amount of total hours of sunshine per day, or effective radiation in general influence production and thus impact yield. Next to light, also other climate factors such as relative humidity, growing season, and wind have an effect on growth. It can be expected that except for temperature, precipitation, light and relative humidity, influences of other factors are minor. However, to arrive at stringent impact conclusions for a climate- yield model, species and site specific analysis is necessary to determine which factors are most influential and thus to be included in such a model. (ibid.)

4.2 Profitability of non- timber goods in forestry investments

4.2.1 Multiple use forestry and carbon sequestration

The goods and services provided by forests provide benefits that need to be taken into consideration in the optimization decision of landholders. The decision criterion for forest project investments commonly acknowledges the benefits that derive from timber production- namely net revenues from selling timber. However, forests provide a variety of non- timber benefits with either a value in use or a value in non use such as scenic beauty, protection of watersheds or carbon sequestration (Bishop, 1998). These non- timber benefits of forests form different compatibilities with timber production as the non- timber benefits are either local or global public goods, whereas timber production is a private good (Nagata, 2004). From a social point of view, a lack of economic incentives for non- timber benefits will lead to an undersupply of the non- timber goods and services (Bishop, 1998). These economic incentives aim at that landholders would consider multiple forest uses in their decision making process on forest investments by determining the investment value (Perman et al., 2003).

Carbon sequestration as non- timber benefit provided by forests can be considered a public good in accordance to the classification of Samuelson (1954). According to Bishop (1998) and Nagata (2004), carbon storage/ carbon sequestration is a pure public good. Other authors like Navarro (2003a) however, consider carbon storage/ sequestration a subject of rivalry and therefore as a common pool resource. Despite this controversy, the line of Bishop (1998) and Nagata (2004) is followed for the research.

As public goods have no market value, non- timber forest products in general and carbon sequestration in specific may be underprovided in case that no compensation is provided for the externalities produced (Bishop, 1998). Hence, landholders do not take these positive external benefits into account in private decision making. Therefore a lack of internalization of these externalities can lead to a suboptimal provision of carbon sequestration from a social point of view (see also Perman et al., 2003). As a consequence, when mitigation of climate change is understood as this positive externality of carbon sequestration, it is likely that mitigation potentials of forests are not sufficiently exploited.

In the case that carbon sequestration is optimally provided, the private optimal decision equals the social optimal decision (Perman et al., 2003), which contemplates the rationale behind, for instance, market- based mechanisms and government interventions in the climate change debate. These different market-based instruments or mechanisms have been created to enable landholders to appropriate the value of non- timber benefits and who will thus provide sufficient carbon storage (see also Ley and Sedjo, 1997a). On the national level, an example for these instruments or mechanisms are PES schemes. On the international level, regulated and voluntary carbon markets provide good examples.

Successful internalization of the externalities according to Van Kooten et al. (1997) takes place when the marginal benefits of carbon sequestration of one carbon unit equals the marginal carbon sequestration costs when an appropriate damage function for increased GHGs is considered (Richards, 1997). As the damage i.e. the consequences of climate change is uncertain (see also Hoen and Solberg, 1997), the main problem is to identify the appropriate value for carbon sequestration services in order to arrive at a socially optimal provision of forest carbon sequestration. Additional revenues, which base upon carbon credits or upon PES, aim at internalizing these benefits to make landholders consider the additional value in their decision making.

Commonly in multiple use forestry, carbon sequestration as non- timber product or service is considered a constraint to the maximisation of timber yield (see also Gregory, 1987; Thompson et al., 1997. As the present study, in contrast, considers carbon sequestration within the maximization of the profitability, carbon sequestration benefits need to be integrated in the decision criteria.

4.2.2 Capital budgeting and decision criteria

Decision making in forestry projects in general is based on efficiency criteria that relate to capital budgeting concepts. These criteria determine which forest project investments maximize the value of the asset i.e. the forestland with the tree stands. These criteria can be classified into the Net Present Value (NPV) and its derived criteria like the Internal Rate of Return (IRR), the payback period or the benefit/cost ratio, as well as into the criterion of the Land Expectation Value (LEV) (see also Navarro, 2003a).

NPV and LEV both determine the optimal rotation age that inherently maximizes profits, and thus determines the financial profitability of an asset. The profitability is based upon a present value approach and upon the discounting of future income streams (Sharma, 1993). This present value approach, deriving from microeconomic consumption theory, is applied in order to value income from different investments (see also Varian, 2006). Income streams from the producer's asset are discounted by a specific interest rate to arrive at the present value used for ranking purposes according to consumption possibilities (ibid.).

The LEV and NPV are based on the concept that the activities on the land generate capitalized payments. Thus, both criteria are based on capital theory, asset theory, and investment theory (Sharma, 1993; Navarro, 2003a). Either criterion determines the rotation age when the investment maximizes the value of the productive asset which is hereby defined as the forestland composed of the land itself and the timber produced. The microeconomic definition of assets applies to forestland as forestry activities generate future income over time which in turn is used for consumptive aims (Navarro, 2003a; Varian, 2006). Investments in forestland assets are only undertaken, according to asset value theory, when the respective forestland produces the highest returns at each point of time (Varian, 2006). At each of these points of time, in line with Fisher's theory on capital and investment, the marginal return of the investment needs to equal the interest rate in order to make the investment in a forestry project profitable (see also Samuelson and Nordhaus, 1995). It can therefore be derived that the decision making process of investing in alternative assets over time describes an intertemporal allocation problem. For forest assets, the marginal return of investment is defined as the marginal return on the forest capital, or as the value growth of the forest (Klemperer, 1996). This marginal return of the forest capital needs to be at least equal to the interest rate that the capital can accrue if invested elsewhere, i.e. the marginal return needs to compensate for the opportunity costs of capital (ibid.). An individual investor therefore will consider an investment as profitable when the marginal return on the forest capital, or the value growth, is equal to the interest rate which is also denominated the minimum acceptable rate of return (MARR) (ibid.).

The two efficiency criteria concerned are based on the same concepts presented above. However, each criterion maximizes the present value of the forestland asset differently. The NPV judges the profitability of a forestry project including the purchase of land as it considers land as a production factor (see also Pereira de Rezende et al., 2005). In that sense, the NPV determines the net difference of discounted costs and discounted benefits of an investment (Sharma, 1993). Present value revenues being greatest, the NPV approach indirectly determines the economic rotation age when the investment in the forestland is maximised. The purpose of the NPV in general is to rank projects of different capital investments. The ranking results from the decision rule that if the discounted cash flow for perpetuate rotations at the discount rate is equal or greater than zero, the investment is accepted (Navarro, 2003a). The LEV is based on the NPV but does not integrate the purchase or selling of the bare land tract (Oderwald and Duerr, 1990; Pereira de Rezende et al., 2005). By this, the LEV considers the forestry activity as such and how profitable the activity on the land is or whether it should be used for another activity. It determines the maximum present value of the forest land as sum of infinite series of all future revenues (Oderwald and Duerr, 1990; Sharma, 1993; Navarro, 2003a). All future rotations, in that respect, are equal regarding their costs and revenues (Navarro, 2003a). In contrast to the NPV, the LEV does not focus on the ranking of projects by determining the discounted net revenues but emphasizes the value of the forestland in perpetuity. The maximum present value of the forestland can be determined by the value in use which is calculated based on the method of the NPV (ibid.). If the maximum value of the forestland does not exceed the market price of the land, forest activities may not be a profitable use of the land. It can be stated that depending on the objective of the research, either criterion is appropriate for decision making in forest investments. Considering that the LEV determines whether the forestry activity is profitable by comparing the asset value concerned to the market price of the land, it may be a stronger criterion as it allows comparisons of asset values with different scales (ibid.).

4.2.3 Joint Land Expectation Value

The original LEV model proposed by Martin Faustmann (see also Faustmann, 1849) treats land as the only fixed capital and bases upon the land rent theory of Ricardo. Ricardo's land rent theory considers soil as the only fixed capital good. The LEV in that sense defines the value of the bare land that can be compared to the market value of the land, and by this indicates profitability of the forestry project.

Linking multiple use forestry to the LEV decision criterion, in line with the joint forestland value by Calish et al. (1978), provides the rationale for the joint land expectation value. The joint forestland value conceptually derives from the original approach to calculate the LEV. The original LEV is adjusted for the present value of the carbon benefits by calculating the non- timber forestland expectation value and linking it to the timber forestland value (Navarro, 2003a; Perman et al., 2003).

According to Perman et al. (2003) regarding multiple use plantations, the inclusion of carbon sequestration as non- timber benefit for infinite rotation plantations can lengthen or shorten the optimal rotation that maximizes profits. The respective outcomes depend on the timber volume function and the value of the non- timber benefits (ibid.). It can be concluded that timber prices and non- timber prices, volume function, the associated plantation costs and the applied discount rate determine the overall joint land expectation value.

4.3   Interim conclusions

Simple yield and growth models can predict potential productivity of forest resources. As described, these models represent the relationship of a tree growth parameter, age, and any site factor. As climatic conditions constitute an important site factor to determine tree growth, previous studies have used climate variables to project potential yield of plantations for specific climatic regions. Based on this, yield and growth models with age and climatic factors as explanatory variables can be used to determine how present climate conditions but also future climate conditions impact tree productivity. In this sense, climate- yield models can be used to estimate present and future yield. These potential changes in yield may consequently alter benefits from forestry projects.

These benefits, according to multiple use forestry, comprise timber and non- timber benefits. As the investment decision is based on the present value of future income streams and associated costs, a joint present value of timber as well as carbon sequestration benefits is an appropriate approach to determine the maximized profits and optimal rotation age for multiple use plantations.

Like previous studies presented in section 3.2.3 and 3.2.4 indicate, the inclusion of carbon revenues can affect the profitability of forest positively and can lengthen the optimal rotation age.

As the value of the joint forestland depends on the volume function, the value for timber and non- timber i.e. carbon revenues, the associated project costs and discount rate; the overall Joint Land Expectation Value is likely to change for alterations in any of these determining factors. Since yield for future climate conditions can potentially change, the value of timber and non- timber benefits might modify accordingly. As a result, climate change induced yield alterations may affect the profitability of forest investments and indirectly the rotation age. Therefore, the LEV can be considered a suitable criterion to analyse the profitability as it is based on successive rotations and allows comparisons of projects with different length.

5   Methodology

To address the research objective of the present study, this chapter provides a thorough overview of the methodology addressed in the analysis. Section 5.1 briefly presents the research area of the case study. Section 5.2 provides a detailed description of the research design regarding the climate- yield model (5.2.1), the profitability model (5.2.2), and concludes on how the former can be integrated with the latter (5.2.3). Section 5.3 presents the data necessary for the analysis and differentiates for tree data (5.3.1), climatic data (5.3.2), and economic data (5.3.3).

5.1   Research area

The Republic of Costa Rica, administratively divided into 7 provinces, 81 cantons, and 470 districts, has a surface area of 51,100 km² and counts with a population of about 4.51 million inhabitants. The country is located in Central America and borders to Nicaragua in the North, Panama and the Caribbean Sea in the East, and the Pacific in the West and South. Central America's climate in general is defined as tropical with a defined rainy season as well as dry season. The latitude of Costa Rica, furthermore, explains the prevailing intertropical climate with high temperatures and abundant rainfall during the majority of the year. Regional differences in climate due to prevalent atmospheric wind circulations, the country's isthmic position, as well as location and altitude of the orographic relief, determine six main climate categories in Costa Rica. These climatic differences allows for the diversity in forest types and biodiversity in the country. (INEC, 2009)

Figure 1 shows the two regions of Costa Rica, the North Pacific region and the Central Pacific region, which form the research area. The Pacific Coast, and in particular the North Pacific region and the North West region of Costa Rica (Guanacaste), are favourable regions for teak plantations due to their climatic and edaphic characteristics (see also Cervi, 2006). The prevailing defined dry season and the low altitudes in these areas explain the great number of reforestation projects in place (Chaves S. and Fonseca G., 2003). Although other regions of the Pacific Coast i.e. the Central Pacific experience less defined dry seasons and higher precipitation, reforestation with teak also occurs in these areas in Costa Rica (ibid.).

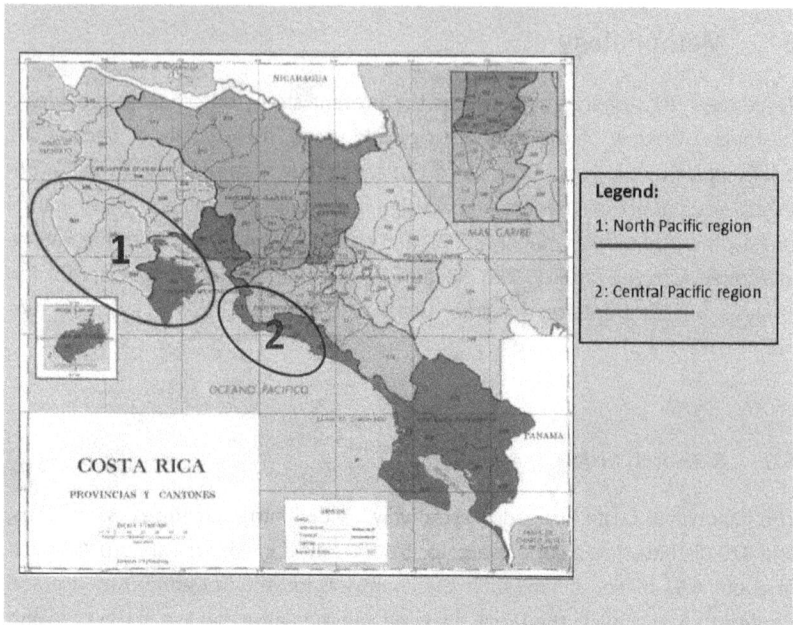

Figure 1: The provinces and cantons of Costa Rica (Source: IFAM, 1985)

The research area covers two distinctive climatic regions. The North Pacific climate differs from the Central Pacific Climate with respect to precipitation and temperature. Distinctive for the Pacific Climate are a greater amount of mean annual precipitation and days with precipitation, together with lower mean annual temperate when compared to the North Pacific region. The North Pacific Region in general is characteristic for its low mean annual precipitation, fewer days with rainfall and higher temperatures. The North Pacific is characterized by a mean annual precipitation of 2072 mm with 131 rainy days and a mean annual temperature of 26 degree Celsius, whereas the Central Pacific counts with an annual average of 174 rainy days, 3621 mm of precipitation and a mean temperature of 24 degree Celsius. (Mena, without year)

In these two regions, a total of ten plantation sites are considered for the case study on teak plantations regarding consequences of a changing climate on the profitability of carbon credit sales.

Figure 2 shows seven of these ten plantation sites that are situated in the North Pacific region, on the Peninsula de Nicoya (see also region 1 in Figure 1). The locations of the seven plantations are Cabuya, Cobano, Bosque 3 in Puerto Carrillo, Norman Quieros in Rio Negro, Nicoya 1 and Nicoya 2 in Nicoya, and Santa Cruz.

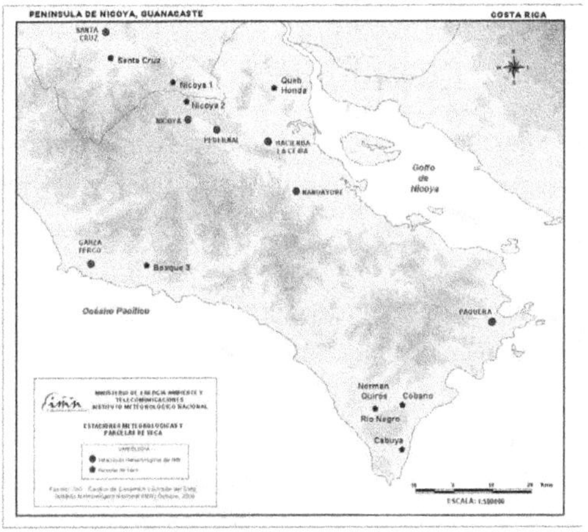

Figure 2: The North Pacific region (Source: IMN, 2009**)**

Figure 3 illustrates the three remaining plantations that are located in the Central Pacific region (see also region 2 in Figure 1). These plantations are Finca Valeria in Aguirre, Finca Tigre in Parrita, and Finca Rios in Quepos.

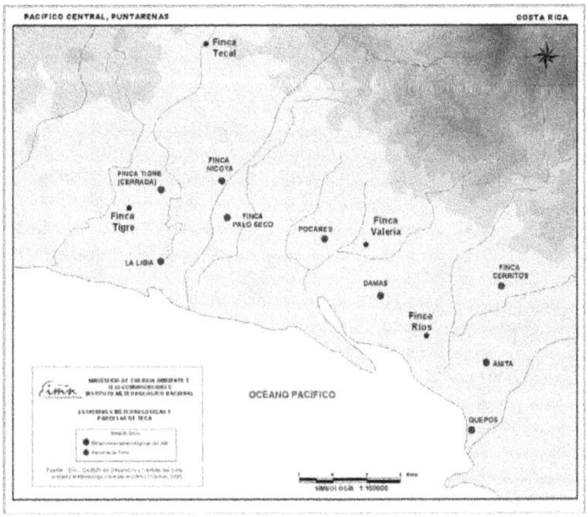

Figure 3: The Central Pacific region (Source: IMN, 2009)

5.2   Research design

The current research comprises an integrated assessment approach in which it links two models in order to analyse the effects of a changing climate on the profitability of carbon credit sales. The respective models are a climate- yield model and a profitability model that are further described in this section. Section 5.2.1 elaborates on the climate- yield model by describing its specification and the respective calibration methods. Section 5.2.2 presents the profitability model, its specification and method of analysis (5.2.2.1), tree volume accounting methods (5.2.2.2), carbon accounting methods (5.2.2.3), as well as accounting methods for benefits and costs (5.2.2.4). Section 5.2.3 then concludes briefly on how the two models will be linked in the analysis. These sections on the research design presented in the following provide the complete methodological framework for the model calibration in chapter 6, and for the model analysis and results in chapter 7.

5.2.1 Climate- yield model

5.2.1.1   Model specification

The climate- yield model to determine which single climate variable or which multiple climate variables have explanatory potential for yield of teak plantations can be specified with a yield- age function that has a mathematical relationship of a log- reciprocal type and can be solved with simple linear regression methods (Avery and Burkhart, 2002).

$$Ln(Y) = b_0 + b_1 * \left(\frac{1}{A} \right)$$
(1)

with
Y   yield parameter
A   tree age
b_0, b_1 coefficients

The climate- yield model for this research constitutes an empirical, individual tree model that is based on the yield prediction function in accordance with Schumacher (1939 cited in Clutter et al., 1983). The basic Schumacher equation is modified for the purposes of the present research to consider climate variables in their linear form as explanatory variables next to age (see also Brack and Wood, 1998). Hence, the analytical model with the following general yield function used in this research can be presented as:

$$Log(Y) = b_0 + b_1 * \left(\frac{1}{A}\right) + b_2 * CL_1 + b_3 * CL_2 + ... b_n * C_n \tag{2}$$

with
$b_0 - b_n$ coefficients
$C_1 - C_n$ climate variables

The climate factors that, in accordance with the conceptual framework, are most relevant in theoretical terms for a climate- yield model are precipitation, temperature, and radiation in general. These general climate variables as presented in equation 3 need to be further specified in the model calibration by choosing the variable with the greatest explanatory potential among the available climate variable specifications like mean annual and total annual precipitation, or minimum and maximum mean annual temperature. Considering that data on radiation is rarely available, radiation is not included. The specific yield- climate function therefore can be presented as:

$$Log(Y) = b_0 + b_1 * \left(\frac{1}{A}\right) + b_2 * CL_{precip} + b_3 * CL_{temp} \tag{3}$$

with
Y   yield parameter
A   tree age
CL_{precip} specified precipitation variable
CL_{temp} specified temperature variable

5.2.1.2   Calibration methods

The climate- yield model is calibrated with linear regression methods. The purpose of the calibration is to determine which specific climate variables regarding
precipitation and temperature have the greatest joint explanatory potential for
the logarithm of the total tree volume. Sequential regression methods and stepwise regression methods are applied to calibrate the climate- yield model.

The sequential regression method bases upon bivariate regressions of each climate variable. In a first step, the inverse of tree age enters the model. This constitutes the base model for the subsequent regressions. In a second step, each of
the climate variable specification enters this general log- reciprocal function of
volume and age. The purpose of these bivariate regressions is to determine the
specified climate variables with the highest R^2 among, first, all precipitation specifications, and second, all temperature specifications. The determined specified
climate variables for precipitation and temperature then enter the full climate-
yield model.

The stepwise regression method is applied to validate the results of the sequential regression method. As in the sequential approach, first, the base model of log
volume and the inverse of tree age is estimated. In contrast however, the stepwise approach determines after each regression the climate variable specification
that contributes most to the overall variance explanation. Therefore, each of the
precipitation (temperature) specifications is added to the base model separately.
In a first step, the precipitation (temperature) specification that adds most to the
overall variance explanation compared to the base model is chosen. The former
base model is enriched with the precipitation (temperature) variable. In order to
choose the second variable, in a second step, the specified temperature (precipitation) climate variable is determined and added to the model based on the same
approach.

The climate- yield model calibrated based on these two methods estimates the
log tree volume based on age and the specified precipitation and the specified
temperature variable which can be applied to predict yield for future climatic
conditions in the analysis.

5.2.2 Profitability model

5.2.2.1 Model specification and method of analysis

The profitability of carbon credit sales in this research is determined with the financial investment criterion LEV. In accordance with the conceptual framework, this financial criterion needs to incorporate timber and non- timber benefits resulting in the Joint Land Expectation Value (LEV$_J$).

The LEV$_J$ assigns the maximum value of the land when dedicated to forestry activities that produce timber and non- timber goods and services. To make the activities on the forest land profitable, the maximum value of the joint forestland needs to exceed or equal the market price of land.

The general Land Expectation Value criterion presented in equation 4 calculates the rotation that gives the land its maximum value based on Navarro (2003b).

$$LEV = \frac{R_T - NPV_T (1 + r_{adj})^T}{(1 + r_{adj})^T - 1} \tag{4}$$

with

$$R_T = P_{tim} * V_{tim}(T) - C_H(T) \tag{5}$$

$$NPV_T = \sum_{t=0}^{t=T} \frac{B_t - C_t}{(1 + r_{adj})^t} \tag{6}$$

with

R$_T$	total annual net revenues at T
P$_{tim}$	timber price
V$_{tim}$	timber volume
C$_H$	harvest costs
B$_t$	benefits in t
C$_t$	costs in t
r$_{adj.}$	risk adjusted discount rate
t	year t of the rotation
T	harvest age

The enumerator gives the future value of the land calculated as the total annual net revenues obtainable at harvest age (equation 5) minus the compounded Net Present Value of the first rotation (equation 6). Timber prices are multiplied with timber volume to obtain total benefits at harvest age T. Total harvest costs are deducted and result in total revenues.

The method applied for the financial analysis comprises the discounted cash flow method. The compounded Net Present Value, in that sense, is calculated as the sum of the discounted benefits and costs for each year of the rotation. This cash flow is capitalized until the end of rotation T with the applied capitalization factor $(1+r_{adj})$. The future value is discounted for the years of the rotation with the factor $(1+r_{adj})^T -1$ to represent the relative value of the land market value. (Navarro, 2003b)

The general LEV formula, as presented above, is modified to result in the LEV_J (see Calish et al., 1978) that accounts for carbon sequestration as non- timber services by combining the LEV for timber (LEV_{Tim}) with the LEV for carbon sequestration (LEV_{CS}) as shown in equation 7.

$$LEV_J = LEV_{Tim} + LEV_{CS} \tag{7}$$

The LEV_J formula includes the total revenues that base upon timber sales as well as carbon credit sales. To obtain the additional carbon sequestration benefits, the volume of carbon sequestration is multiplied with carbon prices as illustrated in equation 8.

$$LEV_J = \frac{[(P_{tim} * V_{tim}(T) - C_H(T)) + (P_{CS} * V_{CS}(T) - C_{CS})] - \left[\sum_{t=0}^{T}(B_t - C_t) * (1 + r_{adj})^{(T-t)}\right]}{(1 + r_{adj})^T - 1} \tag{8}$$

with

P_{CS}	carbon price
V_{CS}	volume of sequestered carbon
C_{CS}	cost of sequestering carbon

44

5.2.2.2 Tree volume accounting methods

The profitability model considers tree volume to derive the subsequent timber as well as carbon sequestration benefits. Therefore, the model accounts for two different volume types, the total volume over bark and the commercial volume. The total volume over bark is utilized to calculate the respective carbon content, whereas the commercial, or merchantable volume, represents timber sales volume.

A double entry model defines volume as a function of total height (H) and diameter at breast height (DBH) as shown in equation 9. This model, the so called Näslund model, is employed to calculate the total volume over bark for an individual tree (in m³) according to equation 10. Following Mora and Gómez (2003), this model proves best to estimate volume of plantation teak trees at the Pacific Coast of Costa Rica when volume models with double entries are considered.

$$V = f(DBH, H) \tag{9}$$

$$V = 0.0000541686 * DBH^2 + 0.0000387435 * DBH^2 - 0.0000244254 * DBH * H^2 + 0.000347646 * H^2 \tag{10}$$

The commercial volume is considered a fraction of the total volume. Equation 11 has been developed by Van Zyl (2005), with reference to Phillips (1995) and teak plantations in Sri Lanka. This defined ratio of total volume to commercial volume is used in the analysis to derive the mean ratio of total volume to commercial volume per tree age for the complete sample.

$$\frac{V_{timb}}{V_{tot}} = 0.949 - \left(\frac{2.557}{DBH^2} \right) \tag{11}$$

with

V_{tot} total tree volume

5.2.2.3 Carbon accounting methods

The value of the carbon sequestration potential in accordance with the conceptual framework is next to the carbon price, dependent upon the carbon stock accounting method, and the revenue accounting methods. The respective methods that will be utilized in the present research are herewith presented.

Carbon stock accounting

The carbon stock method that is applied, considers the potential of the carbon in situ as well as the carbon released at harvest and stored in long- lived products. Therefore, net carbon amounts are derived from carbon content in biomass, in soil, in products over the product's life-span and from release at harvest.

Carbon in total biomass (CC_B)

In order to estimate the amount of biomass carbon stored in one hectare of a teak plantation and derive the respective CO_2 equivalent, commercial tree volume is converted into commercial biomass volume using a species specific wood density (WD) conversion factor.

$$B_{com\_dry}(T) = \sum_{t=0}^{T} V_{com}(t) * WD \tag{12}$$

with
$B_{com\_dry}(T)$ commercial dry biomass at harvest
$V_{com}(T)$ commercial total volume at harvest
WD   wood density

The obtained commercial dry biomass, or also called the dry weight of the merchantable volume, is expanded in a next step using a biomass expansion factors (BEF) as shown in equation 12 in accordance with the IPCC guidelines (IPCC, 2006). The purpose is to account for all non- merchantable biomass components.

$$B_{tot\_dry}(T) = \sum_{t=0}^{T} B_{com\_dry}(t) * BEF \tag{13}$$

with
$B_{tot\_dry}(T)$ total dry biomass at harvest
BEF   biomass expansion factor

With this expansion, all non- merchantable components are accounted for and total carbon in tonnes can be estimated using a species and biomass component specific carbon rate (CR) that with the help of the conversion factor can be converted into CO_2e.

$$CC_B(T) = \sum_{t=0}^{T} B_{tot\_dry}(t) * CR \tag{14}$$

with
$CC_B(T)$ carbon content in biomass at harvest
CR   carbon rate

Carbon stored in soil (CC_S)

For the lack of studies on carbon stored in litter, undergrowth, and soil in teak plantations in the Pacific Coast, results of other regional studies are used to have an approximation of the carbon storage of one hectare.

Carbon released at harvest (CC_R)

The assumptions for the analysis are that trees are immediately replanted after harvest and that thinning and final harvest produce long- lived wood products. Thus, at harvest age, it is assumed that timber is entirely used for wood products and therefore carbon released at harvest comprises the emissions from the immediate release by the non- merchantable volume and the emissions released over life- span.

The carbon released immediately at harvest per individual tree can be calculated as the difference between the carbon stored in total dry biomass and the carbon stored in commercial dry biomass according to equation 15.

$$CC_H(T) = \sum_{t=0}^{T} ((B_{tot\_dry}(t) - (B_{com\_dry}(t)) * CR \qquad (15)$$

with

$CC_H(T)$ carbon content immediately released at harvest

The carbon that is released over the life-span can be calculated using dry commercial volume that equals the proportion of carbon getting stored immediately in the wood products (CC_p). The wood products decay with an annual rate k (0<k<1) over the life-span of the product (Reddy and Colin, 1999). The difference between the immediate storage in the products in year T and the storage potential at the end of the life-span represents the carbon decayed by the product.

$$CC_D(T) = CC_p - \sum_{T}^{T+LS} CC_p(LS)^{(k(-LS))} \qquad (16)$$

with

$CC_D(T)$ carbon content released over product life-span
CC_p carbon content of the product for timber volume at harvest age
LS   life-span of the product
k   decay rate

The net carbon released at harvest at year T is given by:

$$CC_R(T) = CC_H(T) + CC_D(T) \qquad (17)$$

48

Total net carbon (CC_{tot})

The total net carbon captured over the rotation age can be calculated as the yearly increment of the total carbon stored in soil and biomass considering release at harvest and release over the products' live- span. For simplicity reasons it is assumed that increments derive from the carbon sequestration potential of the soil in year 0 i.e. the increments are composed by carbon sequestration due to tree growth.

$$CC_{tot}(T) = [CC_B(T) - CC_S(0)] - CC_R(T)$$ (18)

Revenue accounting method

The revenue accounting method utilized in this research considers the yearly increase or loss (indicated as negative amounts) in carbon and calculates the net annual increase starting off from the carbon sequestration volume in the soil in year 0. The net annual increase in carbon sequestered over the rotation period is multiplied with the carbon price to obtain the carbon benefits for each year. Together with the annual carbon costs, annual carbon revenues are obtained. Similar to Boyland's (2006) dynamic approach, these revenues are together with the timber value discounted for the years of the rotation.

5.2.2.4   Accounting methods for benefits and costs

Costs

For the present research, the costs for timber production equal the costs for carbon sequestration as carbon related costs, such as transaction costs to participate in national PES schemes or the carbon markets, are neglected for simplicity reasons.

The costs that are included can be categorized into production costs (C_P) and harvest costs (C_H). In addition, fixed annual costs (C_F) comprised of costs for telephone and for electricity of the landholder are considered as shown in equation 19. Production costs are divided into initial investment costs (C_I), establishment costs (=equal to afforestation: C_a), and maintenance costs (C_m), including costs for visits by forestry managers. Afforestation costs are taken into account in the end of year 0 of the rotation. Harvest costs consist of logging costs (C_L) and costs of transport to the industry (C_{Tr}) as prices at industry level will be considered in the analysis. Both costs items are multiplied by the commercial volume at year t and do not differ for thinning or final harvest.

$$C_t = C_P(t) + C_H(t) + C_F(t) \tag{19}$$

with

$$C_P(t) = C_I(t) + C_A(t) + C_M(t) \tag{20}$$

and

$$C_H(t) = \left[(V_{com}(t) * C_L) + (V_{com}(t) * C_{Tr})\right] \tag{21}$$

Benefits

Timber benefits (B_{Tim}) are obtained by multiplying the volume of commercial wood at thinning or final harvest (V_{com}) with the price (P_{Tim}) obtainable per cubic meter. The mean commercial wood volume of the number of trees per hectare at tree age t, derived from the mean total volume, is considered as representative for the sample and will be employed in the financial analysis as the base case. Benefits, as shown in equation 22, at thinning year t are considered maintenance benefits that resemble benefits at final harvest when obtained at harvest age T.

$$B_{Tim}(t) = V_{com}(t) * P_{Tim} \tag{22}$$

The maintenance benefits get reduced for the production costs, fixed costs and thinning harvest costs at year t. These are summed and discounted from year 0 until rotation age to arrive at the Net Present Value for the first rotation as indicated on the upper right hand side of equation 8. Instead, final harvest costs (C_H) are deducted from harvest benefits and result in total timber revenues as shown on the upper left hand side of the same equation.

In addition to timber benefits, carbon sequestration benefits are obtained. The research considers two sources of carbon sequestration benefits. Benefits from carbon sequestration are for one part comprised indirectly by the general PES for the first five years of the plantation and enter the Net Present Value equally to maintenance benefits (see equation 8).

The focus, however, is on the direct revenues from the net carbon sequestration of one hectare as discussed in section 5.2.2.2. The amount of net carbon sequestration in CO_2e multiplied with the respective carbon credit price enters the LEV_J calculation as shown on the left hand side of equation 8.

5.2.3 Integrating the climate- yield model with the profitability model

The climate- yield model to be calibrated estimates the log tree volume based on age and on the specified precipitation and the specified temperature variable. Through these specified climate variables, the log tree volume can also be predicted for future climatic conditions as projected by different climate change scenarios.

These climate change scenarios result in projections of mean annual temperature and mean annual precipitation for different scales for the future. Applying these alterations of temperature and precipitation in the calibrated climate- yield model allows projecting yield production scenarios for future climatic conditions that in turn enter the profitability model. In line, the profitability model analyses the discounted cash flow for each of these yield production scenarios. For each case, the Joint Land Expectation Value is determined which are then compared to analyse the possible consequences of a changing climate on the profitability of carbon credit sales for landholders.

5.3　Data

The following section gives an overview of the data needed to carry out the cali-bration of the climate- yield model and the analysis of the profitability of carbon credit sales under a changing climate. This section in accordance with the meth-ods presents tree data, climatic data, and economic data. The first section (5.3.1) addresses all tree related data and thus accounts for the site specific data for teak and data on carbon stock calculations. The second section (5.3.2) presents the available historic climate data for the region as well as the climate change scenar-ios that project future climate. The third section (5.3.3) introduces the economic data for the financial analysis that are benefits, costs, income tax, as well as op-portunity costs.

5.3.1　Tree data

5.3.1.1　Site-specific teak data

The extensive, not publicly available data collections of the INISEFOR (without year-a; without year-b) provide site specific data on teak for the research area. These data collections contain measures of dasometric variables, like total height and DBH, of sampled plantations at different ages and for varying site conditions. This dasometric data has been collected with methods of permanent plots meas-urements over a specific period in time, also called Permanent Plot Method (PPM), and with methods of stem analysis (StA) that in contrast is applied after harvesting. The data collections are used to retrieve the necessary data for the purpose of the research. This comprises information on direct growth parameter such as diameter at breast height over bark and total height. Tree age is subse-quently derived from the calendar year of the measurements or the felling of the tree, in the case of PPM or StA respectively.

The PPM has been carried out on plots of each 500m^2 with varying site quality and different thinning management applied. The site quality is characterised by medium to high class sites. The foresters, who established the permanent plots at plantation sites of different ages and varying stand densities, applied different thinning regimes to measure their effects on growth. The PPM data collections provide average data for trees of plantations per plot dating that date back until 1984 at most.

In contrast, stem analysis is carried out posterior the harvest as special techniques allow retrieving DBH and height for single trees and by this the compilation of data on larger time periods. The present study considers 11 trees of this stem analysis data, with the oldest tree originating in 1952. No information, however, is retrieved about initial stand densities, plot area and management systems.

In total, ten plantation locations are considered that comprise 53 plots differing in site quality and in applied management systems. Table 1 provides a general overview for the site specific teak data with information on locations, plantation plots, measurement method applied, coordinates and elevation. A detailed overview of the plantation plots that provide the site specific teak data is given in Appendix A together with prevailing climate conditions.

Table 1: Overview of teak plantations

Region	Location	Plantation name	# of plots	Period of plots/ tree	Method	Coordinates		Elevation (in m)
						Latitud	Longitud	
North Pacific	Cabuya	Cabuya	10	1989-2003	PPM	9.62	85.09	126
North Pacific	Cobano	Cobano	12	1984-2004	PPM	9.69	85.09	148
North Pacific	Bosque 3 in Puerto Carrillo	Bosque 3	10	1995-2005	PPM	9.91	85.52	123
North Pacific	Norman Quieros in Rio Negro	Norman Quieros	10	1989-1999	PPM	9.68	85.13	180
North Pacific	Santa Cruz	Nicoya 1, Santa Cruz	2	1953-1992	StA	10.24	85.58	91
North Pacific	Nicoya 1 in Nicoya	Nicoya 2 and 3	2	1974-1992	StA	10.2	-85.48	176
North Pacific	Nicoya 2 in Nicoya	Nicoya 4	1	1973-1992	StA	10.17	-85.45	179
Central Pacific	Finca Valeria in Aguirre	Valeria	1	1954-1990	StA	n.a.	n.a.	n.a.
Central Pacific	Finca Tigre in Parrita	Tigre	1	1953-1990	StA	n.a.	n.a.	n.a.
Central Pacific	Finca Rios in Quepos	Rios 1, 2, 3 and 4	4	1952-1991	StA	n.a.	n.a.	n.a.

Source: own elaborations based on INISEFOR (without year-a), INISEFOR (without year-b) and Mora and Toruño (2006)

5.3.1.2   Data on carbon stock calculations

The carbon stocks considered according to the stock accounting method are carbon in total biomass, in soil, and the carbon released at harvest. The respective data needed for the calculation of each carbon stock and thus the overall carbon sequestration potential is presented in the following.

Wood density

According to the guidelines of the IPCC (2006) on basic wood density of tropical tree species, the wood density of *Tectona grandis* ranges from 0.50- 0.55 based on Reyes et al. (1992) with reference to Asia. For this study, the mean of the density range being equal to 0.525 will be used to obtain dry commercial biomass from commercial volume.

Biomass expansion factor

As shown in equation 23, a BEF of 1.5319 is utilized in the research that bases upon the results of Kraenzel et al. (2003) on the proportion of trunk biomass, which is considered equal to commercial dry biomass, to total biomass (see also Keogh, 2005). This expansion factor accounts for leaves, flowers, twigs, branches and roots and therefore can be used to calculate the total dry biomass.

$$BEF = \frac{Biom_{total}}{Biom_{trunk}} = \frac{100}{65.28} = 1.5319 \qquad (23)$$

with
$Biom_{total}$ total biomass in %
$Biom_{trunk}$ trunk biomass in %

Carbon rate and soil carbon

According to Kraenzel et al. (2003) and the results of their study on teak plantations in Panama, tree carbon storage estimates can be obtained based on total dry biomass and an average carbon concentration of teak of 0.495. The same authors estimated an average of 225 tC/ha in the soil profile that is used in the analysis as approximated value.

Decay rate and life- span

For the lack of information on specific decay rates of teak, it can be assumed that timber is used as saw wood which allows applying a default decay rate according to IPCC (2003). This constant annual rate for harvested wood products is based on a default half-life (λ) of the carbon stored in saw wood according to equation 24.

$$k = \frac{\ln(2)}{\lambda} = 0.0198 \qquad (24)$$

with

k   constant annual decay rate
λ default half life for saw wood products (35 years)

Considering the durability of teak timber products, a life- span of years is considered to be over 25 years according to Bhat et al. (2007). However, other informal sources indicate that products have a far larger life- span than 25 years, and therefore the present study applies a plausible life- span of 50 years.

Conversion factor of carbon tonnes into CO_2e

The obtained tonnes of carbon per plantation hectare for biomass, soil and products need to be converted into CO_2 equivalents with the conversion factor of 44/12 to be able to apply carbon prices in the financial analysis.

5.3.2 Climatic data

5.3.2.1   Historic climate data

The analysis uses historic climate data that has been obtained from the National Meteorological Institute of Costa Rica (IMN, without year). The purpose of the research, to investigate the relationship of climate and yield, requires the use of data from on site climate stations to attribute for the varying microclimate among the plantation sites. However, as climate stations are in very few cases established on site or are situated in immediate proximity; appropriate stations that best describe on site climatic conditions need to be selected. In total, five meteorological stations are chosen based on proximity, data availability and on the topographic characteristics of the plantation areas and the climate station surroundings (Retana, pers. comm.). As prevailing precipitation and temperature patterns are affected by, for instance, elevation levels or the existence of mountain ranges, these characteristics of the areas need to be similar to provide representative climate data (ibid.). Table 2 shows which climate stations are chosen to best represent the climatic conditions for the different plantation locations as indicated in Figure 2 and Figure 3 in section 5.1. Stations Paquera, Nicoya, Santa Cruz and Pocares provide monthly precipitation data, and the stations Nicoya, Santa Cruz and Damas supply figures on monthly minimum and maximum temperature. Note that an overview of precipitation and temperature data of these stations for the respective tree plots can be found in Appendix A.

Table 2: Overview of selected climate stations for the plantation locations

Region	Location	Plantation name	Climate station for	
			Precipitation	Temperature
North Pacific	Cabuya	Cabuya	Paquera	Nicoya
North Pacific	Cobano	Cobano	Paquera	Nicoya
North Pacific	Bosque 3 in Puerto Carrillo	Bosque 3	Nicoya	Nicoya
North Pacific	Norman Quieros in Rio Negro	Norman Quieros	Paquera	Nicoya
North Pacific	Santa Cruz	Nicoya 1, Santa Cruz	St. Cruz	St. Cruz
North Pacific	Nicoya 1 in Nicoya	Nicoya 2 and 3	Nicoya	Nicoya
North Pacific	Nicoya 2 in Nicoya	Nicoya 4	Nicoya	Nicoya
Central Pacific	Finca Valeria in Aguirre	Valeria	Pocares	Damas
Central Pacific	Finca Tigre in Parrita	Tigre	Pocares	Damas
Central Pacific	Finca Rios in Quepos	Rios 1, 2, 3 and 4	Pocares	Damas

Source: own elaborations

The monthly average precipitation data are used to calculate total annual precipitation. In order to account for any seasonal effects, mean and total precipitation are also calculated for the dry season and wet season, lasting from May to November and from December to April, respectively. Regarding temperature, both mean annual minimum and mean annual maximum temperature are considered. Table 3 presents an overview of the average of the total annual precipitation, the average on the mean annual minimum temperature, as well as maximum temperature for each climate station per region. The averages for the indicated years of records serve as averages of the historic climate data for two baseline periods- 1960-1990 and 1980-1999- that this overview differentiates for. This differentiation is later needed to apply future climate change scenarios accordingly. The table also indicates the years of records of the data that have been summarized to represent these baseline periods. Note that when lacking the average monthly data, the average monthly data for the entire period of data availability from the station are taken.

Table 3: Overview of historic climate data per region and baseline period

Climate station	Baseline period	Precipitation (in mm)		Temperature (in °C)		
		Average total annual precipitation	Years of records	Average mean annual min. temperature	Average mean annual max.temperature	Years of records
North Pacific						
Paquera	1960-1990	1,968	1974-1990			
Nicoya	1960-1990	2,177	1960-1990	21.42	33	1960-1990
Santa Cruz	1960-1990	1,775	1960-1990	22.55	33.12	1971-1990
AVERAGE		1,973		21.99	33.06	
Paquera	1980-1999	2,132	1980-1999			
Nicoya	1980-1999	2,074	1980-1999	22.8	32.71	1980-1999
Santa Cruz	1980-1999	1,741	1980-1999	22.98	33.06	1980-1999
AVERAGE		1,982		22.89	32.88	
Central Pacific						
Pocares	1960-1990	2,901	1961-1990			
Damas	1960-1990			22.57	30.9	1983-1990
AVERAGE		2,901		22.57	30.9	
Pocares	1980-1999	3,259	1980-1999			
Damas	1980-1999			22.64	31.02	1983-1999
AVERAGE		3,259		22.64	31.02	

Source: own elaborations based on IMN (without year)

5.3.2.2   Climate change scenarios

Climate change scenarios provide the relevant information on future climate conditions that are necessary to project yield production scenarios for the future. These climate change scenarios project mean annual temperature and mean annual precipitation for a specific scale considered. The projections base upon assumptions on emission scenarios regarding demographic, economic and technological aspects that are grouped into four scenario families denominated A1, A2, B1, and B2, and that disregard any additional climate policies. (IPCC, 2007)

The present study applies two sets of climate change scenarios. The first set is based on the regional climate projections produced for the latest Assessment Report of the IPCC by a multi model data set (MMD). The second set to apply relies on the preliminary regional climate projections in Costa Rica by the model 'Providing Regional Climates for Impacts Studies' (PRECIS). The scenarios of each set differ in their scale. The MMD results in projections with a resolution of about 1,000 km (IPCC, 2007), whereas the PRECIS provides projections with a resolution of 50 km or 25 km (MINAE and IMN, 2008).

The climate change scenarios of both models are presented in Table 4. The table shows that the MMD set includes one scenario for the entire region of Central America. The projections assume future emissions according to the emission scenario group A1B[6], and are undertaken for 2080-2099 with a baseline of 1980-1999. According to the median of the number of the MMD models, most of Central America will experience a mean annual temperature change of 3.2 degree Celsius and a general decrease of 9% in precipitation. (IPCC, 2007)

The PRECIS model simulates for regions within Costa Rica. Considering that the research area lies in two different climatic regions, this set of scenarios by the PRECIS model provides two scenarios; one for the North Pacific and the other for the Central Pacific. The assumed emission scenarios for PRECIS are in line with the emission scenario group A2[*], and projections are made for 2081-2100 with a baseline period of 1961-1990. For the North Pacific, the model projects an increase of 4.5 degree Celsius in mean annual temperature, and a decrease in 40%

---

[6] The emission scenario group A1B assumes a very rapid economic growth, a population growth that has its peak around 2050, and the fast introduction of an increasing number of more efficient technologies for all sources. The A2 group, instead, assumes a slow economic growth, high population growth, and slow technological change.

of mean annual precipitation. In contrast, projections for the Central Pacific result in a temperature increase of 3.6 degree Celsius and a positive percentage change in precipitation of 14%. (MINAE and IMN, 2008)

Table 4: Climate change scenarios per model for different regions in Central America

| Model | Emission scenario group | Region | Projections | | Baseline period | Projection period |
			Increase in mean annual temperature (in °C)	Change in mean annual precipitation (in mm)		
MMD	A1B	Central America	3.2	-9%	1980-1999	2080-2099
PRECIS	A2	North Pacific (Nicoya)	4.5	-40%	1960-1990	2080-2100
PRECIS	A2	Central Pacific (Quepos)	3.6	14%	1960-1990	2080-2100

Source: own elaborations based on IPCC (2007), MINAE and IMN (2008)

Considering the environmental heterogeneity of Costa Rica, the PRECIS model with its high resolution is expected to simulate precipitation and temperature patterns in a realistic way (see also MINAE and IMN, 2008), although the MMD can provide reasonable scenarios. The results of the PRECIS scenarios in the analysis will be compared to the results of the MMD scenario to contrast the impact the choice of scenario has on the present analysis.

5.3.3 Economic data

5.3.3.1 Benefits

Timber management and timber production

The financial analysis assumes a standard initial tree stand density of 1111 trees per hectare. As shown in Table 5, thinning is carried out in year 5, 10, and 15, according to what is considered optimal for the region (Meza, pers. comm. a). Although final harvest is considered to be optimal in year 30, it is delayed until year 40 in the analysis to apply yield projection scenarios appropriately.

Table 5: Overview of stand density, thinning regime and final harvest

Activity	Year	# of logged trees	Remaining trees (in #)
Planting	0	0	1111
Mortality	1	0	1000
Thinning 1 (non- commercial)	5	400	600
Thinning 2 (commercial)	10	300	300
Thinning 3 (commercial)	15	150	150
Final harvest	40	150	0

Source: own elaborations based on Meza (pers. comm. a)

According to the thinning scheme, the first thinning at year 5 does not produce merchantable timber. The second and third thinning, as well as the final cut produce teak that can be sold locally at sawmills or directly to purchasers at farm level.

Timber products from teak plantations in general comprise firewood, wood poles, thin wood and bulk wood. Landholders in the North Pacific Region have difficulties to find purchasers for firewood and wood poles produced on teak plantations (teak producer, pers. comm.). Thus, it is assumed for both regions that firewood and wood poles do not generate income and therefore are not considered. Thin and bulk wood products are differentiated according their diameters at harvest age.

Teak prices

Prices for log wood (or round wood) are obtained from a local sawmill that is considered representative for the region. The prices that are presented in Table 6 vary for diameter of the stem as well as quality of the timber. In the present study, only diameter is considered for price variation for simplification reasons. Quality aspects are therefore not taken into account.

Table 6: Teak prices at industry level

Circumference (in cm)	Diameter (in cm)	Prices (US$/m³)*
<50	<15.9	117
50-70	15.9-22.3	140
>70	>22.3	175

Source: own elaborations based on sawmill staff member (pers. comm.)

Carbon prices and Payments for environmental/ecosystem services

Offset prices for plantation afforestation/ reforestation activities averaged in US$ 8.20 per tCO_2e in 2007 on the voluntary market and with this ranged among the highest prices traded for Voluntary (Verified) Emission Reductions (Hamilton et al., 2008).

Reforestation activities in Costa Rica are eligible for payments for environmental services that also apply for teak plantations. According to the Article 2b of the Act Nr. 34371 (MINAE, 2008), reforestation activities receive a total sum of US$ 816 for a period of five years according to the schedule in Table 7.

Table 7: Payment schedule for PES in Costa Rica for reforestation activities

Year	Proportion of total sum per year	PES per year (US$/ha)
1	50%	408
2	20%	163
3	15%	122
4	10%	82
5	5%	41

Source: own elaborations based on Article 2b of the Act Nr. 34371 (MINAE, 2008)

5.3.3.2 Costs

Production costs

Representative production costs for teak plantations in the research area are compiled with the help of information on activity types and respective labour hours in an exemplary financial structure for teak plantations in the Pacific region (CATIE, 2005). Based on this basic structure, cost data have been updated with information obtained during consultations and during desk research. These consultations and desk research retrieve data on prices for maintenance products, plants, equipment, and their service costs, administrative costs, and fixed costs from cooperatives, agricultural centres, forest technicians, producers, ministries, and national insurance institutes. A summary on the production costs per year is given in Table 8.

In year 0, investment costs that include small investments in equipment and afforestation costs occur. Afforestation costs include activities such as site preparation, purchase, transport and planting of the plants, as well as fertilization, and weed control. Maintenance activities in the first years until year 5 differ slightly from year to year in their activities and thus in their corresponding costs. The main activities during the first five years cover fertilization, diversion channels, round firewalls, mowing, and the pruning of suckers. From year 5 on, maintenance activities comprise only mowing and round firewalls light weed control except for years with thinning. In thinning years i.e. in the years 5, 10, 15, activities that incur costs regarding maintenance include marking and logging of the trees.

Table 8: Overview of production costs (in US $) per plantation phase

Plantation phase	Total costs in ¢/ha	Total costs in US $/ha
Investment and afforestation year 0	425,106	763
Maintenance year 1	428,164	768
Maintenance year 2	462,198	829
Maintenance year 3	421,432	756
Maintenance year 4	348,834	626
Maintenance year 5	118,061	212
Maintenance year 10	121,786	219
Maintenance year 15	78,019	140
Maintenance year t	129,744	233
Maintenance year T	70,188	126

Source: own elaborations based on consultations and CATIE (2005)

The cost structure, in addition, includes annual fixed costs for telephone and electricity, as well as visits from forestry managers for the first five years. A detailed financial structure can be found in Appendix B, indicating the cost differentiation for the categories workforce, inputs and services per year.

Harvest costs

Harvest costs differentiate for costs for cutting as well as for transport costs to the farm gate and sawmill. As prices are expressed in log prices at sawmill, these costs need to be deducted from revenues obtained from commercial thinning and final harvest to arrive at the net revenues.

Table 9: Overview of harvest costs (in US $/ m³)

Harvest costs	Total US $/m³
Cutting costs	
Cutting costs per m³	14.58
Transport costs	
Transport to farm gate	8.75
Transport from farm gate to industry (36 km, Nicoya)	17.49
Transport from farm gate to industry (70 km, Nicoya)	23.32
Transport from farm gate to industry (300 km, SJ)	40.82

Source: own elaborations based on Hernández (pers. comm.), teak producer (pers. comm.), and sawmill staff member (pers. comm.)

Data are collected in consultations and resulted in the price scheme in Table 9 that is applied in the analysis. This scheme presents an average cutting cost per m³, and transport costs to the farm gate, as well as transport costs to the sawmill accounting for different distances to sawmills in the region or to the capital. These costs are applied for both study regions.

Taxes

Reforestation projects in Costa Rica are exempted from income tax (Meza, pers. comm. b) and other taxes are not considered for the present study.

5.3.3.3   Opportunity costs

Opportunity cost of capital

The opportunity cost of capital in this analysis is based on the real interest rate that accounts for risk in forestry projects. The real interest rate equals 3.26% using a nominal interest rate of 15.69% and an average annual inflation rate of 12.04% (BCCR, 2008b; BCCR, 2008c).

The nominal interest rate of 15.69% corresponds to the average interest rate for loans in national currency in Costa Rica in 2008 (BCCR, 2008c), and is considered a justified rate as the study focuses on private, non- industrial landholders that take loans for investments. The average annual inflation rate for producer prices including fuels based on monthly indices for the period from 1999-2008 is 12.04% based on (BCCR, 2008b).

The riskless discount rate is adjusted by adding a risk premium of 1% that is considered a plausible premium for forestry investments in Costa Rica (Meza, pers. comm. c), resulting in a risk adjusted discount rate of 4.26% applied in the analysis.

Opportunity cost of land

The opportunity cost of land is represented by the market value of bare land, estimated with prices that landholders would receive for selling one hectare at present. Information on sales prices per hectare are collected for the region Nandayure (province of Guanacaste) and Cabuya (province of Puntarenas) and considered as representative for the study region in total.

To account for the increase of land value close to coastal zones, perceived average land sales prices are divided into three categories according to the distance to the coast. The categories 1,2, and 3 in

Table 10 represent respectively, great, intermediate, and little distance of plots to the coastal area. The average prices given are only indicative since land prices vary substantially in the area up to 1,000 US$/m^2 for land close to coastal areas in touristic regions.

Table 10: Land costs per category in US $/ha

Land category	US $/ ha
Category 1	8,971
Category 2	44,855
Category 3	239,710

Source: own elaborations based on Hernández (pers. comm. b) and hotel operator (pers. comm.)

6 Model calibration

The following chapter presents the calibration of the climate- yield model according to the methods and the available data described in chapter 5. Section 6.1 first introduces the model in accordance with the available data, and second, presents the results of the data analysis. Section 6.2 comprises the calibration methods and their results. In specific, section 6.2.1 elaborates on the sequential multiple regression model and the stepwise regression model, whereas section 6.2.2 presents the final calibrated climate- yield model.

6.1 Model specification and data analysis

6.1.1 Model specification

The climate- yield model, a linear regression model on empirical, individual tree data and historic climate data is calibrated by OLS methods. The model is presented in its general form in equation 25 below. It shows that yield enters the equation as the dependent variable, and age as well as climate variables enter as independent variables.

$$\text{Log(Y)} = b_0 + b_1 * \left(\frac{1}{A}\right) + b_2 * CL_{precip} + b_3 * CL_{temp} \qquad (25)$$

These variables according to the available data are further specified. The yield parameter, entering in its logarithmic form, is represented by the individual tree volume at a specific age, which is estimated based on the DBH and total height (total volume). The independent variables are tree age, precipitation and temperature. Based on the historic climatic data, the regression will consider three specifications for the precipitation variable as well as two specifications for the temperature variable. Regarding precipitation, these are the total annual precipitation (TAP), as well as total precipitation for the dry season (TAP$_{dry}$) or the wet season (TAP$_{wet}$). It has to be noted that the dry season lasts from December to

April, and the wet season from May to November. Concerning temperature, the specifications used are minimum mean annual temperature (MAT_{min}) and maximum mean annual temperature (MAT_{max}).

6.1.2 Data analysis

Complete data was available for 599 observations. Basic descriptive statistics of the variables are shown in Table 11.

Table 11: Basic descriptive statistics

Variable	Mean	Standard deviation	Minimum value	Maximum value	Observations
Total volume (in m³)	0.4485	0.4228	0.0015	2.1695	797
Tree age (in years)	14	8.4	1	40	925
TAP (in mm)	2240	620	1048	4320	872
TAP $_{dry}$ (in mm)	183	172	0	922	872
TAP $_{wet}$ (in mm)	2057	520	1033	3956	872
MAT $_{max}$ (in °C)	32.81	0.75	30.33	34.12	723
MAT $_{min}$ (in °C)	22.85	0.46	21.1	23.78	723

Source: own elaborations based on data retrieved from IMN (without year), INISEFOR (without year-a), and INISEFOR (without year-b)

Prior the regression analysis, square root transformation to correct for skewness and kurtosis are applied to all three precipitation variables in order to approximate a normal distribution as recommended, for instance, by Lewis-Beck et al. (2004). The variables tree age and total volume are furthermore transformed into its inverse and its logarithmic form respectively, according to the functional form of the general model. All other variables enter as given in the function.

Table 12 shows the Pearson's correlation coefficients of all variables. The coefficients indicate that each independent variable is significantly correlated with the dependent variable on a 1% significance level. The Pearson's correlation coefficients display that the inverse of tree age (Age_inverse) is negatively correlated with the logarithm of the total volume (Log volume). This seems plausible as any volume variable is negatively correlated to the inverse of age, as volume increases with age. All precipitation variables are positively correlated with the log volume, whereas total annual precipitation in its transformation (TAP_sqrt) and log volume result in the highest pair wise correlation. The positive correlation of precipitation and log volume suggest the positive relationship that can be expected according to the theoretical framework. However, the correlations of temperature with log volume indicate an inconclusive relationship as maximum temperature is negatively correlated with the log volume, and minimum temperature is positively correlated with the log volume. Of both temperature variables, maximum temperature shows a higher correlation with log volume.

The correlations between the explicatory variables with each other, which are also presented in Table 12, are relevant in a sense as they show the low correlation of temperature with precipitation variables. This suggests that multicollinearity may not be a problem in the model. The remaining illustrated correlations coefficients are not further relevant.

Table 12: Pearson's correlation coefficients of all variables

Variables	Log volume	Age_inverse	TAP_sqrt	TAP$_{dry}$_sqrt	TAP$_{wet}$_sqrt	MAT$_{max}$	MAT$_{min}$
Log volume	1						
Age_inverse	-0.8118*	1					
TAP_sqrt	0.3774*	-0.1339*	1				
TAP$_{dry}$_sqrt	0.3510*	-0.1547*	0.6765*	1			
TAP$_{wet}$_sqrt	0.3315 *	-0.1045*	0.9695*	0.4842*	1		
MAT$_{max}$	-0.2662*	0.0548	-0.2725*	-0.2115*	-0.2582*	1	
MAT$_{min}$	0.1517*	-0.2176*	-0.2248*	-0.1212*	-0.2220*	0.3473*	1

* p< 0.001

6.2 Calibration methods and results

6.2.1 Sequential multiple regression model and stepwise regression model

6.2.1.1 Sequential multiple regression model

The sequential regression method divides two steps to calibrate the climate- yield model. In a first step, bivariate regressions are carried out to determine which specifications of the precipitation (temperature) variables have the greatest prediction potential for the dependent variable. This determination is based on the criterion on how much the model gains in the explanation of the log volume variance. To further adjust for the number of explanatory variables in the model, the adjusted R^2 is subsequently used as decision criterion.

Table 13 shows the summarized results of the bivariate regressions that also include the regression of the inverse of tree age and log volume.

As indicated, all variables are significantly correlated with the log volume on a significance level (p) of 1%. The simple model based on log volume and the inverse of tree age has a great explicatory potential of the variance as the high adjusted R^2 of 0.66 suggests.

Table 13: Bivariate regression results

Dependent variable	Independent variable	Adj. R2	F		p
Log volume	Age_inverse	0.66	(1, 795)	1536.08	p < 0.001
Log volume	TAP_sqrt	0.14	(1, 744)	123.55	p < 0.001
Log volume	TAP$_{dry}$_sqrt	0.12	(1, 744)	104.51	p < 0.001
Log volume	TAP$_{wet}$_sqrt	0.11	(1, 744)	91.86	p < 0.001
Log volume	MAT$_{max}$	0.07	(1, 598)	45.6	p < 0.001
Log volume	MAT$_{min}$	0.02	(1, 598)	14.08	p < 0.001

Regarding the precipitation variables, the highest adjusted R^2 with 0.14 is found for total precipitation. Concerning the temperature, maximum temperature appears to have a better, however small, explanatory potential for the variance of the log volume.

In a second step, these two specified variables with the highest adjusted R^2 enter the basic model composed of the log volume and the inverse of tree age resulting in the model presented in equation 26.

$$Log(V_{tot}) = b_0 + b_1 * \left(\frac{1}{A}\right) + b_2 * \sqrt{CL_{TAP}} + b_3 * CL_{MAT_{max}} \tag{26}$$

Adding TAP$_{sqrt}$ and MAT$_{max}$ to the basic model of log volume and the inverse of age, results in a gain of the explicatory potential of the model variance as suggested by the increased adjusted R^2 of 0.722 presented in Table 14. This table provides an overview of the regression results of the sequential multiple regression model. Each of the variables is significantly correlated with the log volume at a 1% significance level. The coefficients indicate the relationship between the explanatory and dependent variable as expected from the Pearson's correlation coefficients whereas precipitation is positively, and maximum temperature negatively correlated with log volume. The relatively high absolute t- values suggest that the sign of the true value is not different from the estimate which confirms the relationship between dependent and independent variables. Notwithstanding, it seems that temperature has a far stronger impact on log volume than precipitation.

Table 14: Regression results of the sequential multiple regression model

Sequential multiple regression		Explanatory variable	β	Standard error	t	Confidence interval$_{0.95}$	
Adj. R^2	0.722	Constant	4.7908*	0.239	5.17	2.971	6.61
F	(3, 595)	Age_inverse	-8.6412*	0.239	-36.13	-9.111	-8.172
	518.81	TAP_sqrt	0.0203*	0.003	5.88	0.014	0.027
Obs.	599	MAT$_{max}$	-0.1846*	0.027	-6.94	-0.237	-0.132

* $p < 0.001$

6.2.1.2   Stepwise regression model

Stepwise regression methods are applied to calibrate the climate- yield model that is compared to the preliminary outcomes of the sequential regression model. As in the sequential multiple model, log volume and the inverse of tree age form a basic model. After this step, the climate variable specifications are added individually and the results are compared for their potential to add to the variance explanation.

As can be derived from Table 15, the total precipitation of the dry season, in contrast to the results of the sequential model, is added. This precipitation specification showed greater gains in the adjusted R^2 of the model than when the other precipitation variables were added. Regarding temperature, adding maximum mean annual temperature to the basic model showed a higher increase in the adjusted R^2 than adding the minimum mean annual temperature.

As in the case of the sequential model, all variables are significant at a significance level of 1%. Further, the relationships support the results from the Pearson's correlation coefficients, whereas the t- values indicate the correct sign of the estimate in accordance with its true value.

Table 15: Regression results of the stepwise regression model

Stepwise regression		Explanatory variable	β	Standard error	t	Confidence interval$_{0.95}$	
Adj. R²	0.718	Constant	5.9397*	0.876	6.78	4.22	7.659
	(3, 595)	Age_inverse	-8.7749*	0.24	-36.64	-9.245	-8.305
F	508.38	TAP$_{dry}$ _sqrt	0.0197*	0.004	5.04	0.012	0.027
Obs.	599	MAT$_{max}$	-0.1970*	0.027	-7.44	-0.249	-0.145

* $p < 0.001$

It can be concluded, that the stepwise regression favours the inclusion of total precipitation for the dry season than of total annual precipitation. However, it can be also deducted that adding the temperature specification afterwards, leads to an adjusted R^2 of the calibrated model that is slightly lower than of the model estimated with the sequential multiple regression method. This may suggest that the stepwise regression captures the joint explanatory potential incorrectly. Considering that the adjusted R^2, however, do not vary substantially between the models, and acknowledging that the coefficients are not differing to a great extent, it is plausible to employ both methods to calibrate the climate- yield model. In the following, the preliminary model results are taken from the results of the sequential regression model.

6.2.2 The final climate- yield model

Following the preliminary regression analysis based on the sequential regression methods, the predictive capability of the model is examined. As shown in Figure 4, a scatterplot of predicted values of log volume vs. observed values of log volume suggest a good fit of the model as expected from the regression results.

However, a few outliers can be detected for values less than -2 as illustrated in Figure 4. The examination of these outliers showed that these are in all cases observations with very low total volume at the initial ages of the plantation plots. As outliers can distort the regression coefficients, their deletion can improve the regression results (Lewis-Beck et al., 2004).

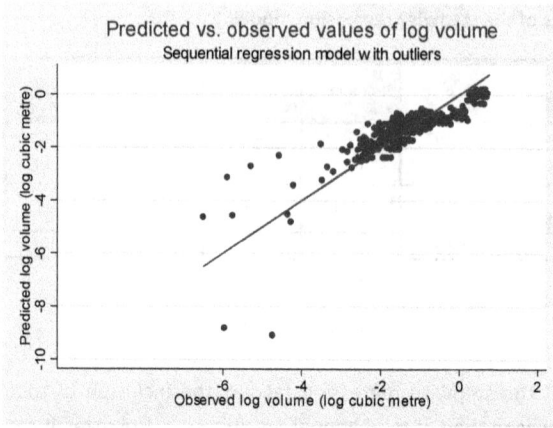

Figure 4: Predicted vs. observed values of the sequential regression model with outliers

Although information can be lost with the deletion of outlier observations, it can be considered a justified measure for the present analysis as there is a high number of observations in total. Figure 5 shows the improved fit of the model after deleting the most obvious outliers.

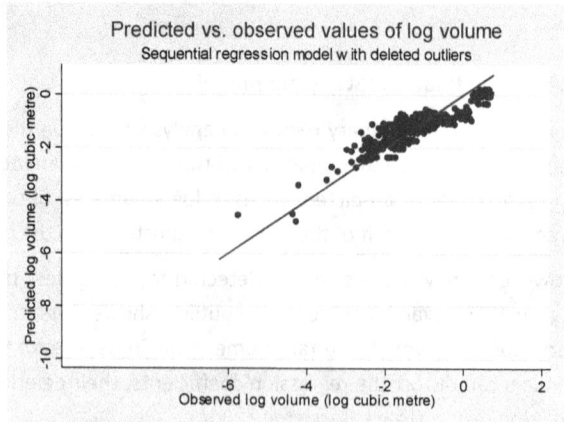

Figure 5: Predicted vs. observed values of the sequential regression model without outliers

Ensuing the deletion of the outliers, the model is calibrated once more with the sequential multiple regression methods. Table 16 presents the summarized regression results of the sequential multiple regression model with deleted outliers. It shows that compared to the preliminary model prior the outlier observation, the model increases in its predictive capability (Adj. R^2=0.792) as the regression coefficients are assumed to be less distortive. As before, the coefficients continue to be significant and indicate the true value of the sign. However, as the value of the coefficients changes slightly, the weight of individual coefficients in explaining the log volume alters; giving more weight to the inverse of tree age and less to precipitation and temperature.

Table 16: Regression results of the sequential multiple regression model (deleted outliers)

Sequential multiple regression		Explanatory variable	β	Standard error	t	Confidence interval$_{0.95}$	
Adj. R^2	0.7916	Constant	4.6753*	0.713	6.56	3.275	6.076
F	(3, 588)	Age_inverse	-10.4583*	0.243	-43.08	-10.935	-9.982
	749.09	TAP_sqrt	0.0163*	0.003	6.1	0.011	0.022
Obs.	592	MAT$_{max}$	-0.1695*	0.021	-8.27	-0.21	-0.129

* p < 0.001

In combination with the outlier deletion, a robust regression is carried out to improve the fit of the model for further influential data (see also Rousseeuw and Leroy, 1987; Yaffee, 2002). As

Table 17 shows, regressing with this robust method results in the same variable coefficients, overall significance of the model and p- values as without the robust method (see Table 16). However, using the robust regression gives the correct standard errors and t- values in case of misspecification of the model (see also Long and Freese, 2006). It can be found that the standard error and t- values change in particular for the inverse tree age. Notwithstanding, these changes have no further implications for the calibrated model.

Table 17: Regression results of the robust adjusted sequential multiple regression model

Robust sequential multiple regression		Explanatory variable	β	Robust standard error	t	Confidence interval$_{0.95}$	
R2	0.7926	Constant	4.6753*	0.96	4.87	2.79	6.561
F	(3, 588)	Age_inverse	-10.4583*	0.341	-30.7	-11.127	-9.789
	427.93	TAP_sqrt	0.0163*	0.003	5.56	0.011	0.022
Obs.	592	MAT $_{max}$	-0.1695*	0.027	-6.23	-0.223	-0.116

* p < 0.001

Hence, the final climate- yield model calibrated with sequential multiple regression methods, as well as robust methods, can be presented as in equation 27. Note that the final regression results of STATA as well as outcomes prior the final regression can be found in Appendix C.

$$Log(V_{tot}) = 4.6753 - 10.4583 * \left(\frac{1}{A}\right) + 0.0163 * \sqrt{CL_{TAP}} - 0.1695 * CL_{MAT_{max}} \qquad (27)$$

The determined climate- yield model allows estimating yield based on age and climate variables. In order to validate for the model's explanatory power, ensuing the mean of the log volume per tree age of the 790 observations is plotted against the predicted values of the model with the respective standard deviations. The detailed information on the mean total volume per tree age of the sample is found in Appendix D. Figure 6 shows the deviation of the mean predicted values from the mean observed values in the beginning until year 3. From year 3 until about year 19, the predicted values approach the observed values very close, indicating that model outcomes for this period give good estimates. However, from year 19 on, the predicted values deviate increasingly from the observed values, in particular from year 23 on. Figure 7 illustrates this in better detail.

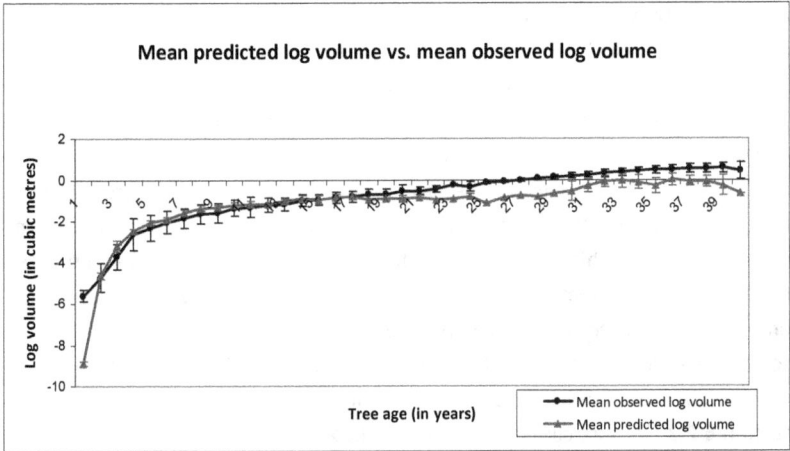

Figure 6: Predicted mean log volume and real mean log volume per tree age

These deviations may be due to the available number of observations per tree age. Only 2.8% and 15.4% of the observations for volume exist for the tree age groups of 1-3 years and of 23-40 years respectively. Therefore, the high percentage of the observations that provide volume data per tree age within the years 4 and 22- namely 81.8%- supports the greater explanatory power of the model for the respective years.

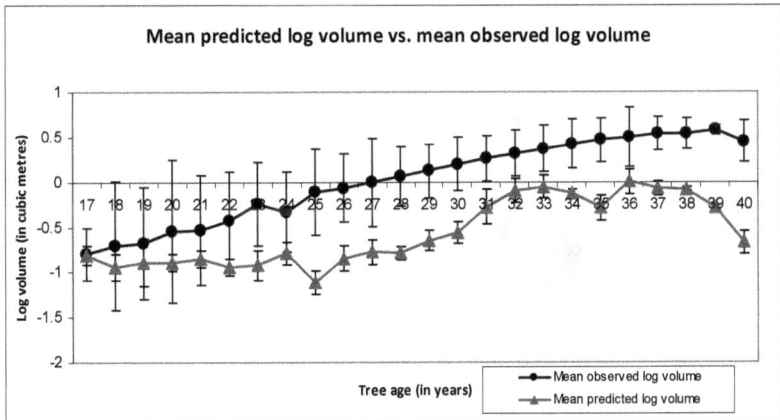

Figure 7: Predicted mean log volume and real mean log volume per tree age (detailed Fig. 6)

As the climate- yield model underestimates the log volume in particular for trees older than 22 years, the direct use of the outcomes of the calibrated model for the financial analysis- that is the estimated log volume with historic climatic as well as future climatic conditions- would lead to distorted values of timber and carbon sequestration benefits after year 22. However, the emphasis for the climate- yield model's application lies on determining the change of produced volume under historic climatic conditions to the one under future climatic conditions. Considering this emphasis, the change in produced volume can be determined in an approximation by using percentage changes in the estimated log volume, which are then transferred and applied to the mean log volume of the observed data. To be more specific, the log volume is first estimated with the climate- yield model using historic climate data, i.e. the final model described in section 6.2.2. Second, climate data from climate change scenarios are used to estimate further log volume data. The percentage change in the estimated log volume is further applied to the mean log volume of the observed data to better account for the volume after year 22. However, as the percentage change rely on underestimated log volume for the later years of an individual tree; it may be plausible that the effects of future climate on yield can be underestimated or overestimated. Therefore the volume data calculated with the percentage change and real data, in particular after year 22, still needs to be considered with caution when applied in the financial analysis as it could lead to erroneous conclusions on the profitability of timber and non- timber benefits over the years.

7 Model analysis and results

The analysis of the profitability and its results are subsequently addressed in the following sections of this chapter. Section 7.1 analyses the effects of future climate on total tree volume, here presented as volume production scenarios (VPSs), in accordance with the calibrated climate- yield model (7.1.1). Furthermore, the implications of these VPSs for timber and carbon sequestration, resulting in volume scenarios (VSs), are made explicit (7.1.2). Section 7.2 analyses and provides the results on the profitability of timber and carbon benefits based on the established VSs. Section 7.2.1 addresses the profitability of timber and carbon benefits under each VS in general, whereas section 0 examines the profitability of carbon credit sales in specific. Section 7.2.3 presents the sensitivity analysis. The chapter on model analysis and results concludes with section 7.3 that provides interim conclusions prior to the discussion and conclusions in chapter 8.

7.1 Volume production scenarios and their respective volume scenarios

7.1.1 Volume production scenarios

The calibrated climate- yield model allows the estimation of log volume per tree age using mean climate data for the determined climate variable specifications. As a result, the model can be applied to project different volume production scenarios (VPSs) depending on the mean climate data used as input. These VPSs comprise first a benchmark VPS that is based on historic climate. Second, they include VPSs for future climate according to the two climate change scenarios considered in the analysis. The production scenarios have the purpose to calculate the percentage change of yield estimates under present climate and yield estimates under future climate. These percentage changes will be further used to examine timber volume and volume of carbon sequestration at present and in future accordingly.

The benchmark VPS grounds in the mean historic climate data summarized in Table 18 for both climate regions and for two different baseline periods. The two baseline periods considered, 1960-1990 and 1980-1999, are relevant since the climate change models that provide the climate change scenario projections operate on these two different baseline periods. As the purpose is to apply these projections on temperature and precipitation to historic climate, the latter needs to consider the same baseline periods as the scenarios.

Table 18: Summarized historic climate data for both baseline periods indifferent of region

Climate Variable	Base 1960-1990	Base 1980-1999
TAP	2,205	2,302
MAT_{max}	32.34	32.26

Source: own elaborations based on IMN (without year)

To arrive at the benchmark VPS, the climate- yield model is used to estimate the yield for individual trees from age 1-40 with equation 28, using the summarized historic climate data for the overall research area presented in Table 18.

$$V_{tot} = Log\left[4.6753 - 10.4583 * \left(\frac{1}{A}\right) + 0.0163 * \sqrt{CL_{TAP}} - 0.1695 * CL_{MAT_{max}} \right] \qquad (28)$$

The results are presented in Figure 8. As two baseline periods exist, present yield estimates result in two benchmark VPSs for the entire research area. Although the numerical values do not substantially differentiate, in the following both VPS are presented for completeness as VPSs for future climate derives from either of these benchmarks.

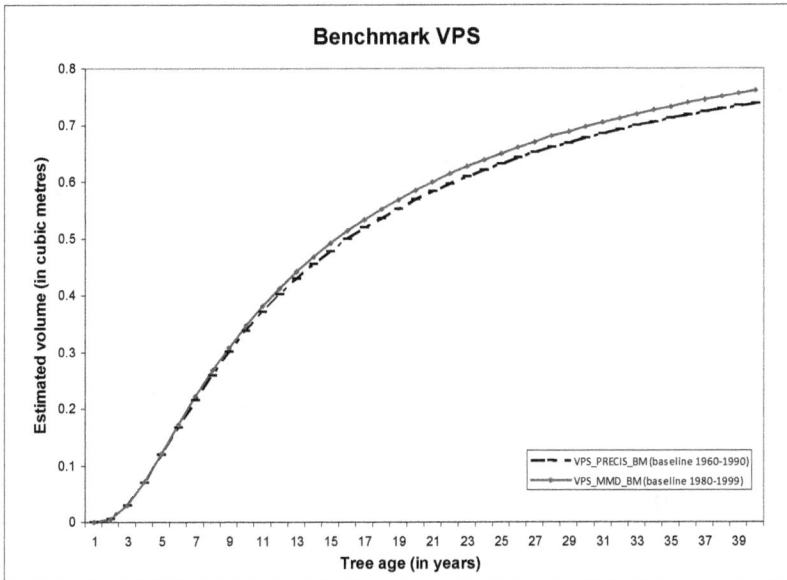

Figure 8: Benchmark VPSs with baseline 1960-1980 (PRECIS) and 1980-1999 (MMD)

Equation 28 is also employed to arrive at the VPSs for future climate. In contrast to the benchmark VPSs that use summarized historic climate data for both regions, the VPSs for future climate use the climate data adjusted for the projections provided by the climate change models considered- MMD and PRECIS. The projections presented in chapter 5 for both models are applied to the historic climate data in accordance with the baselines.

Table 19 gives an overview that first comprises the summarized historic climate data per region for both baseline periods. Second, it shows the projections made by the MMD and PRECIS model for each region. The climate regions distinguished are the North Pacific and the Central Pacific, further denominated region 1 and region 2 respectively. Third, it demonstrates how the projections, using the historic climate data, translate into the estimations for future temperature and precipitation. Note that projections by climate change models are made for mean annual variables. Although the present research uses TAP and MAT $_{max}$ in the cli-mate- yield model, it can be assumed that the projections also apply for these variable specifications as, regarding precipitation, percentage changes are pro-jected. With respect to temperature, it is plausible to apply projections in mean annual surface air temperature to maximum temperature data as there is no spe-cific information available on the behaviour of minimum and maximum tempera-ture under these scenarios.

Table 19: Overview of historic climate data, and climate change projections per region

Region	Model	Historic climate according to baseline period	Projection	Future climate according to baseline period
		PRECIS		
		Baseline 1960-1990		Baseline 2080-2100
	TAP	1,973	-40%	1,184
North Pacific (Region 1)	MAT $_{max}$	33.06	4.5	38
		MMD		
		Baseline 1980-1999		Baseline 2080-2099
	TAP	1,982.43	-9%	1,804
	MAT $_{max}$	32.88	3.2	36
		PRECIS		
		Baseline 1960-1990		Baseline 2080-2100
	TAP	2,901	14%	3,307
Central Pacific (Region 2)	MAT $_{max}$	30.9	3.6	34
		MMD		
		Baseline 1980-1999		Baseline 2080-2099
	TAP	3,259.15	-9%	2,966
	MAT $_{max}$	31.02	3.2	34

Source: own elaborations based on IMN (without year); MINAE and IMN (2008)

Table 19 also shows the different implications of climate change scenarios for the regions. As beforehand mentioned, the PRECIS model provides projections per region, and the MMD projects future climate conditions for the entire research area. Projections for temperature result in an increase in temperature following a homogeneous pattern over the regions. Notwithstanding, the PRECIS model indi-cates that region 1 will experience a greater mean warming than region 2. The projections regarding precipitation, however, are rather heterogenic. Whereas MMD projects an overall decrease of 9%, PRECIS results in projections for region 1 that predict a drop in total precipitation of 40% compared to an increase of 14% in region 2. Considering these projections together with the parameterization of the climate- yield model, one can assume that yield is declining in the future for all regions. However, region 2 may present an exception as the PRECIS model exclusively for this region projects an increase in precipitation that, in turn, may result in a possible yield increase.

To confirm these assumptions, the VPSs for future climate using the values for the future climate per region and model as input to equation 28, are generated in the following. Figure 9 shows these VPSs for the MMD projections (VPS_{MMD_1} and VPS_{MMD_2}) and for the PRECIS projections (VPS_{PRECIS_1} and VPS_{PRECIS_2}) that are altogether contrasted to the benchmark VPS (VPS_{MMD_BM}, VPS_{PRECIS_BM}). The figure also indicates the percentage changes from the benchmark VPS to the respective future VPSs.

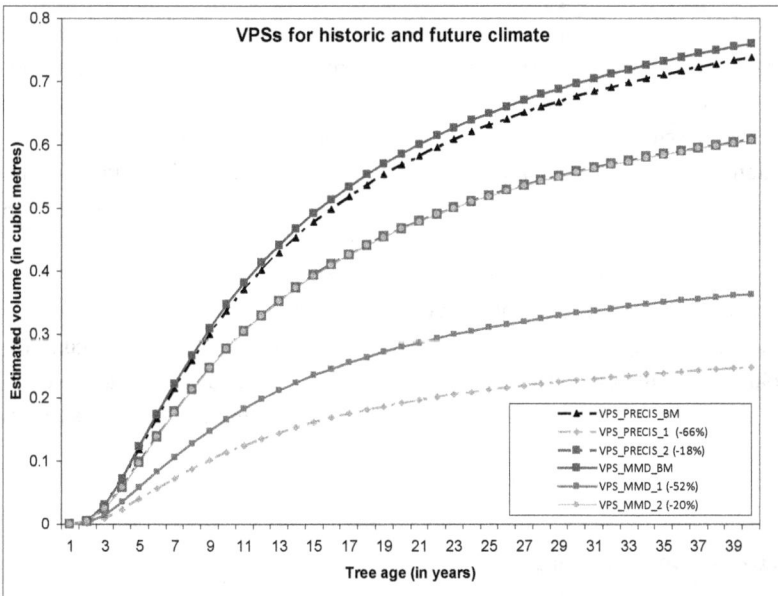

Figure 9: Yield projections per region and climate change projection

The VPSs illustrated in Figure 9 show that the greatest decline in yield can be expected in region 1 compared to region 2, independent of which model provides the projections. The projected changes for region 2 do not vary substantially according to PRECIS or MMD projections, with a decrease in volume of -18% or -20% respectively. However, differences in projected changes in volume are considerable for region 1 as the PRECIS model results in much higher projected volume change-namely of -66%- than the MMD for Central America with a projected decrease of 52%. It can be assumed that this high negative change in yield under PRECIS for region 1 is due to lower precipitation and higher temperature.

The results show that in all climate change projections, each region will experience a decrease in yield when compared to the base case, confirming the assumption made for nearly all regions. Notwithstanding, it contrasts the hypothesized yield increase in region 2 under PRECIS projections. The joint effect of higher temperature and positive precipitation predicted by PRECIS surprisingly leads to nearly the same yield decline as in the case of less warming and negative precipitation as projected by the MMD. This indicates that the impact of future temperature may be the reason for negative alterations in yield. At the same time, the results suggest that positive precipitation can moderate this negative impact of temperature only to some extent. These conclusions are in accordance with the parameterization of the climate- yield model in which temperature has a greater and negative impact on yield than precipitation, which is positively related to log volume but with less weight. As temperature is projected to increase and precipitation is very likely to decrease in nearly all regions, either single variable results in the overall decline of volume.

7.1.2 Volume scenarios

The analysed VPSs translate into implications for merchantable timber volume and volume of carbon sequestration. As each volume type is derived from the total volume projected in the VPSs, these volume production scenarios and their respective percentage changes to their benchmark cases can be applied in order to derive the necessary volume scenarios (VSs). These volume scenarios thus are the result of integrating the VPSs with the volume calculations of timber volume and volume of carbon sequestration for the mean volume per tree. As

Table 20 shows, the VSs are in accordance with the VPSs, except that there is only one benchmark case for the historic climate to which the future volume scenarios are compared to in the financial analysis. For the future climate, again two projections per region are differentiated. To arrive at the VSs presented in

Table 20, the percentage changes from section 7.1.1 are employed with the mean total volume of the tree sample for each. This subsequently alters the calculated timber volumes and volumes of carbon sequestration. Therefore, prior to the application of the percentage changes and thus the integration of the VPSs, timber volume and volume of carbon sequestration need to be calculated for the mean total volume in general, i.e. for historic climate. The calculations, in accordance with the methods of section 5.2.2.2 and 5.2.2.3, are in the following presented in more detail.

Correspondingly, the merchantable timber volume per tree is calculated by applying the ratio between total volume over bark and timber volume per tree. It has to be noted that the application of the ratio is necessary, as the VPSs provide volume data but not data on DBH on which equation 11 bases upon. Therefore, it is necessary to derive this ratio for each tree age, which is based on the mean of total volume and the mean commercial volume calculated with equation 11. The resulting mean ratio of total volume to timber volume per tree age is applied to arrive at the merchantable timber volume per tree. To make this data on individual tree level useful for the profitability analysis, the timber volume per tree is multiplied with the total trees that remain on one hectare of land at year t according to the thinning regime applied. By considering the total number of trees, total merchantable volume accounts for a reduction in volume per hectare due to thinning in year 5, 10, and 15.

In turn, the calculation of the volume of carbon sequestration requires taking into account the uptake in biomass, accumulated over time, and the release of carbon at harvest time. Soil carbon is herewith considered constant over time. Regarding biomass, once the tonnes of CO_2e in biomass per tree are calculated, the thinning regime is considered in the same way as for timber volume to arrive at estimates that are representative on the scale of one hectare. Regarding carbon released at harvest, first carbon released per tree at harvest time is derived, considering the carbon loss of the differential between total and commercial timber volume. In the same way as for biomass, this carbon loss per tree is multiplied with the number of trees per hectare according to thinning regime. As for carbon released over the product's life- span, the differential between the carbon content of the product at harvest time and after a life- span of 50 years is calculated and projected accordingly for one hectare.

Table 20 indicates the implications of the VPSs for the VSs by showing the total amounts of volume regarding timber or carbon sequestration for one hectare of a plantation with trees at the age of 40. This example illustrates the decline in both volume types according to the future climate projection compared to a benchmark volume scenario for historic climate. A detailed overview on the volume amounts per tree age according to VSs can be found in Appendix E.

Table 20: VS for total timber volume and volume of carbon sequestration (rotation year= 40)

Volume scenario (VS)	VS_{BM}	VS_{PRECIS_1}	VS_{PRECIS_2}	VS_{MMD_1}	VS_{MMD_2}
Underlying VPS	$VPS_{MMD\_BM}, VPS_{PRECIS\_BM}$	VPS_{PRECIS_1}	VPS_{PRECIS_2}	VPS_{MMD_1}	VPS_{MMD_2}
Merchantable timber volume					
Mean commercial volume (in m3/ha)	232.84	78.36	191.68	111.39	185.72
Volume of carbon sequestration					
Total accumulated CO2e soil and biomass (in t/ha)	339.88	114.38	279.8	162.59	271.09
Total CO2e released at harvest (in t/ha)	-257.44	-86.64	-211.93	-123.16	-205.34
Net CO2e (in t/ha)	82.44	27.74	67.87	39.44	65.76

Source: own elaborations

7.2 Profitability of timber and carbon benefits

The profitability model determines the financial profitability of teak plantation projects acknowledging carbon sequestration services next to timber sales benefits under present and future climate. To determine this profitability, the analysis applies the volume scenarios of section 7.1.2 and calculates the Joint Land Expectation Value in accordance with the methods in section 5.2.2. The maximization problem is presented in equation 29 below.

$$\max_{T} LEV_j = \frac{\left[\left(P_{tim} * V_{tim}(T) - C_H(T)\right) + \left(P_{CS} * V_{CS}(T) - C_{CS}\right)\right] - \left[\sum_{t=0}^{T}(B_t - C_t) * (1 + r_{adj})^{(T-t)}\right]}{(1 + r_{adj})^T - 1}$$

$$(29)$$

For each VS, the LEV_j is maximised with discounting cash flow methods. Furthermore, the analysis differentiates four schemes of benefits under each VS. These schemes allow for taking into account the different benefit components in the analysis. The schemes are defined into the first that only considers timber benefits (S1) or the second (S2) that includes next to timber benefits also carbon sequestration benefits (CS) from carbon credit sales. The third (S3) and the fourth (S4) scheme, in addition to timber or timber and CS benefits respectively, consider also PES. Note that the PES, in contrast to the other benefit components that are volume related, enter the model as benefits considered in the compounded NPV. For more details, Appendix F provides the overall cost and benefit structure for a plantation including PES until year 40 that is used to calculate the compounded NPV. Considering the differentiation for these schemes in addition to the VSs, the analysis in total will result in 20 maximization problem cases. Each maximized LEV_j is compared to the determined market value of the land to conclude on the profitability of all schemes under each VS. An illustration of the model can be found in Appendix G, where the LEV jointly for timber, CS and PES under the benchmark volume scenario is presented.

7.2.1 Profitability of all schemes under each VS

The analysis assumes an even-aged, pure teak plantation of one hectare in an infinite rotation model with a maximum rotation period of 40 years. Land use conditions at the beginning and the end of each rotation is bare land, i.e. afforestation takes place at the beginning of each rotation. Carbon is sequestered in soil and biomass from year 1 on and is stored with a decaying rate in timber products after harvest. Costs, timber and carbon benefits, as well as the discount rate are constant over time. In addition to timber and carbon benefits, the analysis also includes benefits in form of PES. Accounting occurs at the end of each year, beginning in year 0. The discount rate applied in the analysis is with 4.26% adjusted for risk (based on BCCR, 2008b; 2008c). Timber generates either 78,000 ¢/m³ (140 US $/ m³) and 97,500 ¢/m³ (175 US $/ m³) of trees with diameter over 15.9 and over 22.3 cm respectively (based on sawmill staff member, pers. comm.). Carbon sequestration generates 8.20 US $/ton CO_2e from carbon offset sales (Hamilton et al., 2008). PES benefits comprise 816 US $ distributed over the first five years of the plantation (MINAE, 2008).

The results for all benefit schemes under each VS are presented in

Table 21 and Figure 10.

Table 21 shows a positive maximized LEV_j in all cases for an optimal rotation age of 8 years, except for scheme 1 and scheme 2 under the VS_{PRECIS} for region 1. The determined optimal rotation age in the cases for the negative maximized LEV_j increases to year 32, for which the least negative value can be found.

Table 21: Maximized LEV$_j$ (in 1,000 ¢/ha) per benefit scheme under present and future VS

Scheme/ VS	VS$_{BM}$	VS$_{PRECIS\_1}$	VS$_{PRECIS\_2}$	VS$_{MMD\_1}$	VS$_{MMD\_2}$
S1- timber	11,555	-1,202	8,070	1,272	7,565
S2- timber and CS	12,038	-1,164	8,468	1,503	7,951
S3- timber and PES	13,095	15	9,610	2,811	9,105
S4- timber, PES and CS	13,578	177	10,008	3,042	9,490

Source: own elaborations

Figure 10 illustrates the results for the maximized LEV$_J$ for all 20 cases and indicates those that are profitable as they surpass the threshold of the plotted market value of the land with 5 Mio. ¢/ha. The figure clearly demonstrates that the inclusion of carbon sequestration in general (S2 and S4) increases the maximized LEV$_J$ that only considers timber benefits (S1) or timber benefits and PES (S3) respectively. However, increases are not substantial. In contrast, the inclusion of PES (S3 and S4) increases the maximized LEV$_J$ compared to S1 or S2 by far more. This suggests that the highest LEV$_J$ under each VS is obtained for the benefit scheme 4 that includes timber and carbon benefits, as well as PES.

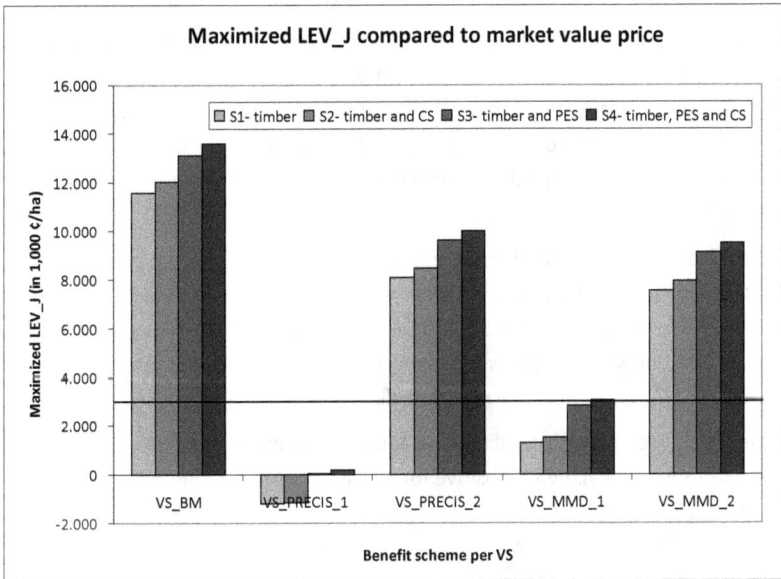

Figure 10: Maximized LEV$_J$ per benefit scheme under each VS compared to market value price

Considering the decline in yield that the VPSs determine, and its subsequent implication for the VSs for future climate, it is not surprising that the LEV$_J$ is highest for all cases under historic climate conditions when compared to the respective cases under future climate, independent of the volume scenario considered. As expected, the figure shows that the Joint Land Expectation Value in region 1 will be substantially less than in region 2 under either climate change scenario. Furthermore, it pinpoints that these lower LEV_J in region 1 do not surpass the market value of the land in contrast to region 2. This suggests that forest projects in future independent of the benefit scheme considered will become unprofitable in region 1 and will become less profitable for region 2 when compared to the present.

7.2.2 Profitability of carbon credit sales within and among the VS

Following the general results on the profitability of all schemes under each VS, the schemes S2 and S4 are further examined. First, the analysis presents the results for added profitability through the inclusion of CS benefits next to timber benefits (with or without PES) within each VS. Second, the profitability of schemes 2 and 4 is analysed and presented for each VS compared to the benchmark VS.

Table 22 presents the absolute increases in the maximized LEV_J when comparing S2 to S1 or S4 to S3 respectively. Except for region 1 under the VS_{PRECIS_1}, absolute increases are the same when S2 and S4 are considered. For VS_{PRECIS_1}, these increases are, however, different which can be explained with the concerning maximized LEV_J being negative in S1 but slightly positive in S3 as

Table 21 shows. Notwithstanding, the added profitability due to the inclusion of CS benefits within each VS is positive for all cases as Table 22 indicates.

Table 22: Added profitability through CS inclusion within each VS

Scheme/ VS	VS_{BM}	VS_{PRECIS_1}	VS_{PRECIS_2}	VS_{MMD_1}	VS_{MMD_2}
S2/S4	483,106	38,425 (S2) 162,585 (S4)	397,709	231,114	385,333

Source: own elaborations

Table 23, in turn, presents the absolute decreases in profitability for each future VS when compared to the benchmark VS as expected in accordance with the VS for future climate. The table therefore suggests under which future VS landholders can expect least negative impacts on the profitability when CS benefits are included in the maximization of the LEV_J. According to the values of the absolute increases within each VS, the decreases are the same for S2 or S4, except for VS_{PRECIS_1}. The analysis of the added profitability of CS benefits provides results that are concordant with the conclusions on timber and carbon benefits in general. These are, considering the inclusion of CS benefits, that region 2 will experience least negative impacts when compared to the benchmark case.

Table 23: Added profitability of CS benefits for future VS

Scheme/ VS	VS_{PRECIS_1}	VS_{PRECIS_2}	VS_{MMD_1}	VS_{MMD_2}
S2/ S4	-444,681 (S2) -320,521 (S4)	-85,397	-251,992	-97,773

Source: own elaborations

Both comparisons presented, within each VS and for each future VS compared to the benchmark, suggest that carbon sequestration benefits in general add profitability compared to timber benefits only under the climate conditions in question. At the same time, the added profitability is adversely affected by changing climate conditions in the future. The decrease in profitability from present climate to future climate is always less than when only timber benefits (with or without PES) are considered. This suggests that least adverse effects of climate change occur when carbon sequestration benefits are included (S2 and S4), in specific, in region 2 under the VS_{PRECIS}.

7.2.3 Sensitivity analysis

The sensitivity of the Joint Land Expectation Value under the volume scenarios for present and future climate with regards to the profitability of carbon credit sales is analysed for several key factors. These key factors include the risk adjusted discount rate, timber prices, carbon prices, and land costs. The analysis evaluates the sensitivity to a simulated change of 40% in prices and discount rate as an example. A percentage rate of 40% is chosen, as it can represent a plausible decrease or increase in carbon prices and timber product prices in future. Regarding the risk adjusted discount rate, a change in 40% can simulate how a rate closer to zero would affect the results in contrast to higher discount rates normally applied in discounted cash flow analyses. The application of other, possible percentage rates is considered beyond the scope for the present sensitivity analysis. In addition, the analysis looks at alternative market value prices for land.

7.2.3.1   Discount rate

Figure 11 displays how the discount rate alters the outcomes of the financial analysis for each benefit scheme under the VSs. As expected, an increase (decrease) in the discount rate leads to lower (higher) absolute LEV_J values when compared to the benchmark case for the discount rate, with $R_{adj.}$ equal to 4.26%. Although the pattern of added profitability of the schemes within each VS does not alter, the overall profitability of a project can change for the discount rate being low enough. As the figure shows, forest projects in region 1 under the VS_{MMD} can become profitable when the according benefit scheme- namely S3 and S4- is considered. The opposite effect takes place when too high discount rates are applied which turns formerly profitable projects into non- profitable ones as in the case of region 2 under VS_{MMD} for the S1 and S3 benefit scheme. Hence, the inclusion of CS benefits in these cases is crucial for the overall profitability when compared to the market value price. It can be concluded that the changes in the LEV_J values are substantial with alterations in the discount rate. This suggests a high sensitivity of the financial indicator to the discount rate.

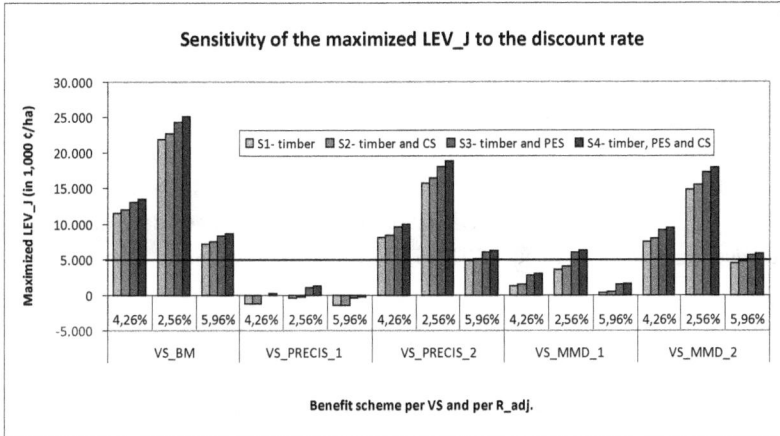

Figure 11: Impact of altering discount rates on the LEV

7.2.3.2 Carbon prices and timber prices

In addition, the analysis tests the effects of altering carbon prices and timber prices on the LEV$_J$ in order to account for uncertainty in future prices on timber as well as carbon markets. Both, timber prices and carbon prices are positively related to the LEV$_J$.

Figure 12 shows that carbon prices affect the financial indicator only slightly and thus lead to a small increase in the absolute value of the LEV$_J$. It can be concluded that the alternative carbon prices considered are not substantial in their impact as to change decisions on a project, which can be seen in Figure 12. The cases, in which projects are not considered profitable when compared to the land market value price in the reference case, continue to be unprofitable independent of whether carbon prices experience an increase or decrease. The analysis of sensitivity to carbon prices also shows that the added profitability of CS benefits for future VS follows the same pattern as in the reference case which indicates that the changes in profitability towards future VSs compared to the benchmark are volume related and not price related.

Considering the low impact of rising carbon prices, together with the focus of the research on carbon credit sales profitability, it has been further examined which carbon price would be necessary to make the forest projects that are most adversely affected by climate change, profitable. The most adversely affected forest projects can be found in region 1 under the VS_{PRECIS} as shown, for instance, in Figure 10. A forest project in that region according to the climate change projections will, when CS benefits are included (=S2), have a negative maximized LEV_J of about 1,164,000 ¢/ha. The carbon price necessary to turn this into a profitable project- i.e. that raises the LEV_J to at least 5 Mio. ¢/ha- has been determined with iterative methods to be about 330 US $/ t CO_2e.

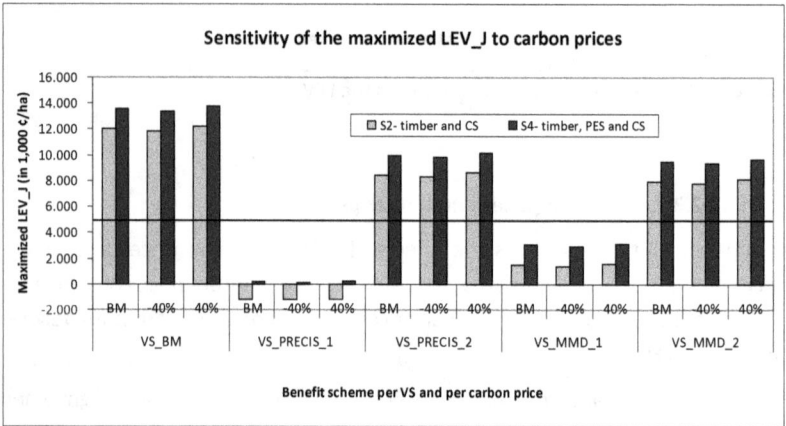

Figure 12: Impact of carbon prices on the profitability of the project

The Joint Land Expectation Value and thus the profitability of carbon credit sales are as expected, and in contrast to carbon prices, considerably sensitive to timber prices. Figure 13 shows that changes in timber prices lead to substantial alterations in the absolute values of the LEV_J. In contrast to carbon price changes in this sensitivity analysis, alternative timber prices have an effect on decision outcomes about a project's overall profitability. The figure illustrates that a decrease of timber prices of 40% will result in unprofitable projects in all cases, independent of whether the project is profitable under the benchmark case or not. In contrast, an increase of the same percentage leads to such a high LEV_J that forest projects with any benefit scheme considered for region 1 under the VS_{MMD} become profitable. Figure 13 also suggests that projects in region 2, in turn, even continue to be profitable when the market value price is increased.

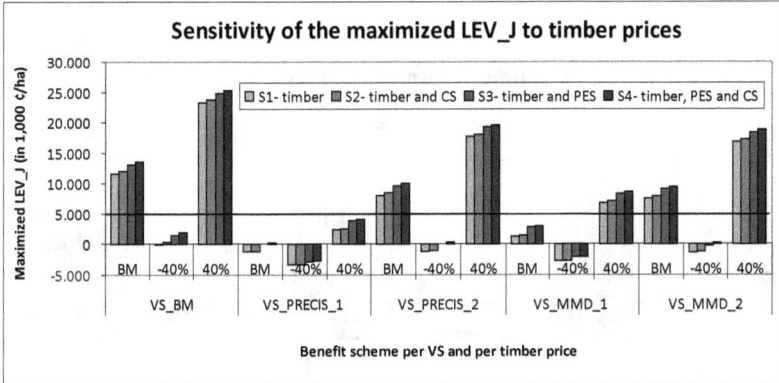

Figure 13: Impact of timber prices on profitability

7.2.3.3   Land costs

As the decision on the overall profitability relies on the considered market value price of the land, the sensitivity analysis also includes an evaluation of how an increase in land costs affects the profitability. The reference case uses a market value of land that has a great distance to coastal zones. As a consequence, alternative values considering less distance result in higher market prices. Until the sensitivity analysis, the market value of land used is 5 Mio. ¢/ha for land in category 1. The sensitivity analysis applies the market value of land of category 2 and category 3 with 25 Mio. ¢/ ha and approximately 134 Mio ¢/ha respectively. For either category 2 or 3, none of the project is profitable holding all other factors constant as none of the LEV_j in the reference case exceeds 25 Mio. ¢/ ha. However, as the choice of discount rate is crucial, it is further examined how a lower discount rate affects these results. From Figure 14 can be concluded that even with a discount rate of 2.56% forest projects on land of category 2 are not profitable except for the case that considers all possible benefits under the VS_{BM}. Thus, it can be stated that the profitability of a forest project depends to most extent on the market value price.

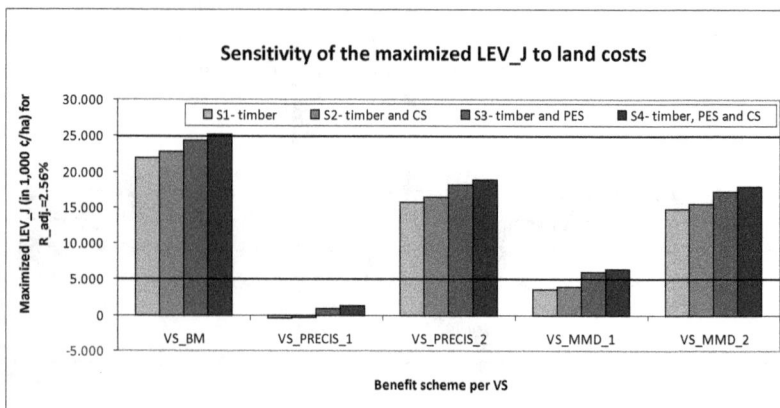

Figure 14: Changes in profitability considering low and intermediate with $R_{adj.}=2.56\%$

The main conclusions derive from the sensitivity analysis in accordance with the results presented above. First, the choice of the appropriate discount rate greatly determines the LEV as well as the profitability, and thus the outcome of the analysis. Low discount rates, i.e. low opportunity costs of capital, favour projects with benefits in the long-term as it is the case with forestry. Second, carbon prices have a substantially lower impact on the financial indicators than timber prices. As a consequence it can be concluded that uncertainty about carbon market prices is not as relevant for the profitability of carbon sequestration projects at present and at future climate conditions. Instead, timber prices determine the profitability of a forestry project. Third, the profitability of a project greatly is determined by the market value price that the LEV_J is compared to. As shown, if land costs rise above the lowest value, none of the cases under the scenarios will result in profitable projects unless the discount rate is lowered sufficiently. It is also plausible that with higher timber prices, the same results can be achieved.

7.3   Interim conclusions

The analysis of the profitability of carbon sequestration in teak plantations for present and future climatic conditions arrives at the following main issues: First, the analysis shows that the inclusion of carbon sequestration benefits increases the LEV_J and thus the profitability of the forest project. Second, the inclusion of carbon sequestration benefits, however, has no substantial impact on the profitability. This derives from the great importance that timber prices play in the profitability as shown in the sensitivity analysis. In addition, the inclusion of only PES to timber benefits leads to higher LEV_J than when CS benefits are included. Third, the best profitability can be achieved when timber benefits, PES and CS benefits are considered. Fourth, considering the decrease in yield under all future climate scenarios, which has been derived with the climate- yield model, future profitability when carbon is included will decrease for all regions. The least decrease in profits is experienced when PES next to timber is considered. Nevertheless, different estimated climate conditions have different impact on the profitability of teak plantation projects. The analysis suggests that region 2 under the VS_{MMD} will have least adverse impacts of climate on the profitability of teak plantation projects including carbon sequestration benefits. In contrast, region 1 under both future VSs, but in particular for VS_{PRECIS}, will be most adversely affected in future and carbon credit sales would need to achieve prices of about 330 US $ to compensate these effects in that particular case.

8   Discussion, conclusions and recommendations

This research investigates the effects of climate change on the profitability of carbon credit sales by addressing the following research questions: what are the effects of climate change on tree productivity; and what is the impact of potentially changing tree productivity under climate change on the profitability of carbon credit sales? These research questions were addressed in a case study on *Tectona grandis* plantations that are located on the Pacific Coast of Costa Rica. The method of an integrated assessment allows a demonstration of links between climate change and productivity on the one hand, and changing productivity and the profitability of carbon credit sales on the other hand. The models that have been applied to assess this relationship include a tree yield model based on climate factors, and a profitability model that integrates timber and carbon sequestration benefits. The outcomes of the research suggest that climate change impacts forest resources as the IPCC states (Easterling et al., 2007), and as scientific research by e.g. Alig et al. (2004), Sohngen et al. (2007), Reilly et al. (2007), and Boisvenue and Running (2006) confirms. The research furthermore finds that carbon credit sales in general augment profitability as indicated e.g. by Gutierrez et al. (2006). Nevertheless, the overall profitability in future will depend on the response of tree productivity to a changing climate, with all other factors held constant.

8.1   Discussion

The research supports the position that climate change can affect forest productivity negatively as is found for example by Clark et al. (2003). It has to be noted that climate change in the research is accounted for by considering changes in temperatures and in precipitation only. Leaving out the consideration of elevated levels of CO_2 or other factors caused by a changing climate that impact tree productivity, may have effects on the research outcomes. Despite the necessity to include these additional factors, uncertainty of the combined effect of these climate change factors on tree productivity prevails as previous studies show. For instance, there exist great ambiguities whether the joint effect of CO_2 on the one hand, and temperature and precipitation on the other hand, may affect forest productivity negatively (Clark et al., 2003), or positively (Reilly et al., 2007).

In addition to elevated CO_2 levels, a complete climate change impact analysis would also need to consider factors other than the level of GHGs or changes in temperature and precipitation, such as the frequency and intensity of extreme climate events.

The theoretical log- reciprocal climate- yield model based on Schumacher (1939, cited in Clutter et al., 1983; Brack and Wood, 1998) serves to estimate total volume based on the climate variables considered. The model's results suggest that increased temperature together with altered precipitation levels has a negative effect on total volume. However, the model does not account for other climate factors like radiation or relative humidity or other site factors such as soil properties, topography, or density (Pandey, 1996; Bebarta, 1999). Including these factors, the climate- yield model would gain in explanatory potential and its results may be more reliable. The model in general has methodological shortcomings due to the combination of exclusion of variables, missing data and its consequences for the variables considered, as well as insufficient ecological modelling skills.

The missing data, for instance, concerns soil related data and data on topography. Further, the available data showed shortcomings as indicated by the results of the estimated log volume with the calibrated climate- yield model. The available tree data observations were concentrated in the age group from 3-23 despite the large number of total observations for tree volume per age. This may be the reason for biased results in the estimations from year 23 on. In addition, it can also be assumed that the lack of data on density and thinning regimes may have led to the underestimation of the volume, as appropriate grouping of the data for these variables was not possible. In addition, linear regression methods that were applied to calibrate the model may erroneously represent the impact of the climate variables on volume as OLS assumptions may not be sufficiently fulfilled and thus have possibly led to the deviation of predicted values from the observed values.

Due to these methodological shortcomings, the results suggest simple relationships of climate variables and tree productivity that partly confirm the findings of Pandey (1996). The research supports the author's result on the positive relation of precipitation and yield, but cannot elaborate on how precipitation affects yield beyond a certain optimum level. Regarding temperature, the detected negative impact of changing temperature on yield contrasts with Pandey's (1996) results on mean maximum temperature and yield, but for instance, supports the findings of Westfall and Amateis (2003) or Clark et al. (2003). However, despite that these ambiguities regarding the temperature- yield relationship exist and that would further call for site and species specific research, the results on the relationship of temperature and yield presented here can be considered plausible. In conclusion, the findings can therefore make a contribution to define the behaviour of yield concerning temperatures for the species teak in Costa Rica. These determined individual relationships of precipitation and temperature with log volume suggest that temperature and precipitation jointly affect tree volume negatively when the projections for future climate are considered. The individual effects are both negative as well. Precipitation, although positively related to log volume affects future tree productivity negatively as projections signal negative changes in precipitation amounts, except for the Central Pacific region. Temperature instead, considering its negative relationship with tree volume based on the model, also affects tree productivity negatively as projections indicate homogenous increases over the regions of mean annual temperature. As a conclusion, the results suggest that, individually as well as jointly, temperature and precipitation in future may affect tree productivity negatively with the exception of the Central Pacific region where precipitation can have positive effects when considered individually. This confirms the importance of the temperature effect on tree productivity as found by Clark et al. (2003).

The profitability model that integrates the concept of multiple use forestry regarding carbon sequestration (Bishop, 1998; Perman et al., 2003), with capital budgeting criteria can be considered a suitable model to determine the profitability of forest activities in general, and in specific, when carbon credit sales are acknowledged. The resulting Joint LEV criterion that is determined with the profitability model, serves to analyse the profitability of forest projects with varying timber and carbon benefits due to climate change induced volume alterations. As the formula used for the LEV_j calculations is commonly used in Costa Rica, the results of this thesis is of use to local researchers as it allows a comparison to findings of other studies undertaken in the region.

Results confirm the findings of Huang and Kronrad (2006), Cubero and Rojas (1999), and Gutierrez et al. (2006) on increasing profitability of plantations when CS benefits are included. The increase in maximized LEV_j determined in this thesis under each volume scenario also supports the research findings of Stainback and Alavalapati (2002), which indicate a possible additional profitability to the landholders due to an increasing LEV when CS benefits are acknowledged. At the same time, the thesis results suggest that carbon sequestration benefits have no substantial impact on the profitability in contrast to timber benefits as Locatelli and Pedroni (2003, p.80) support by stating: "Whatever the hypothesis for the future price for tCER, carbon revenues seem to be nothing more than a small side revenue, with the real, core business being timber marketing."[7]

The analysis of the research strikingly indicates that carbon benefits add less to the profitability of timber sales than PES, which are commonly viewed as too low in their amounts. However as expected, the results confirm that in line with the research of the above mentioned scholars, the highest profitability is achieved when timber, CS benefits and PES benefits are combined.

The research maintains and supports the finding on added profitability due to CS benefit inclusion. Further, it contributes by investigating the implications of future volume scenarios in accordance with climate change scenarios for the profitability of CS benefits. The approach of an integrated assessment as described by Lindner et al. (2002ª), Cannell (1996), and Saxe et al. (2001) proves valuable for the present investigation as site specific vegetative response of teak trees to a changing climate is linked to the profitability of CS benefits. By this, the research contributes substantially to existing site and species specific integrated assessments on climate change that consider CS potentials, as integrated assessments according to the literature presented do not include carbon markets so far, and thus do not link to the profitability of carbon credit sales under changing climate.

The results of the integrated assessment, which connects the climate- yield model with the profitability model, suggest that the forest activity under future climate in general is decreasing in its profitability, often below the respective market value of the land. This suggests that forest activities, regardless of which benefits are included, will be unprofitable in the regions considered in the analysis. Specifically, the research finds that the North Pacific region in Costa Rica, according to the local PRECIS climate change projections, but also to the global projections by MMD, will suffer the greatest decline in profitability. The Central Pacific region in turn, will need to cope with only moderate decreases in yield and thus decreased profitability. This suggests that climate conditions that already cause negative

---

[7] Locatelli and Pedroni (2003, p. 80). 'Accounting methods for carbon credits: impacts on the minimum size of CDM forestry projects.' Global Change Group, CATIE, Turrialba.

impacts in future will intensify and result in further adverse effects (see also MI-NAE and IMN, 2008). For instance, the North Pacific is a region with a distinct dry season that already can impact tree growth negatively if dry seasons intensify as a result of higher temperatures and longer seasons. Therefore, the increase in temperature predicted and the additional decrease in precipitation are likely to cause substantial negative impacts on teak growth in the region. Despite the methodological limitations of the climate- yield model, the results seem to confirm this behaviour. The analysis, in contrast, suggests that the Central Pacific region, which at present is viewed as less favourable for teak in accordance with Chaves S. and Fonseca G. (2003), will experience less adverse effects. Thus, this region in the future could become more attractive for forest investments including carbon sequestration. The overall results of volume changes and hence profitability, however, do not all confirm the hypothesis made on the impact of climate change scenarios. The hypothesis that a changing climate possibly also leads to an increase of volume and thus profitability due to the projected increase in precipitation for the Central Pacific region, could not be confirmed. As the volume production scenarios showed, the effect of an increase in precipitation is not strong enough to counteract the adverse impact of an increased surface air temperature.

Examining the effects of a changing climate on the profitability of carbon credit sales as a specific benefit, the analysis analogously to the pattern of overall project profitability implies that profitability of CS diminishes as total volume figures decrease in any future climate change scenario. It can also be concluded that despite the adverse effects that climate change will have on total volume, and thus timber volume and volume of carbon sequestration, the inclusion of CS benefits in the calculation of the financial profitability will arrive at higher profitability than when exclusively timber sales are included. As such, the negative impacts of a changing climate on the forest plantations can be counteracted with CS benefits. However, the analysis also showed that these benefits are not high enough to make the forest activity worthwhile unless future incomes are valued higher. The applied carbon stock accounting methods in line with Swisher (1997) lead to results on volumes of sequestered carbon per hectare that can be compared to other studies of the region. Findings of a final soil and biomass stock of approximate 1165 t CO_2e (318 t C) that correspond to the presented accumulated uptake of 340 t CO_2e (93 t C), are similar to those of Kraenzel et al. (2003) with 351 t C for the final stock of Panamanian teak plantations. The volume results, based on the referred carbon stock method, may imply that the low CS benefits may be due to the carbon revenue accounting method, i.e. induced by the discount rate or due to the carbon price as such. Boyland (2006) advocates a specific discount rate for carbon sequestration benefits that is different from the timber discount rate. The results based on the applied carbon price further indicate that carbon market prices may be too low to make the forest activities worthwhile. For example, the carbon price that in this research is found to compensate for the negative effects of climate change in the area with the worst projections for volume, centres about 330 US $ per t CO2e. This shadow price of carbon can be compared to the carbon price of 376.81 US $/t CO2e estimated by Boyland (2006) with discounting methods for new plantations. These figures, together with estimates on marginal abatement costs by other studies, indicate that carbon market prices may be not high enough to provide sufficient incentives to internalize the externalities, and thus to make carbon sequestration profitable. These other studies, although for other research purposes, state for instance that the carbon sequestration potential of plantations can be provided in the short term for around 27.25 US $/t CO2e (Strengers et al., 2008), or 7- 55 US $/t CO2e (Sohngen and Brown, 2008). The mentioned studies show a great deal of variance in carbon prices and carbon credits on the markets in general. For example, credits on the voluntary markets for forestry projects ranged from 1.80 US $/t CO2e to 300 US $/t CO2e for 2007 (Hamilton et al., 2008). Despite, its weighted average price of 8.20 US $/t CO2e for plantations, and also other figures on credit prices, for instance, on the CDM market where CERs for registered projects were traded for €12-13 at the end of 2008 (Point Carbon, 2009), are in general too low when compared to the studies.

Furthermore, it has to be noted that the present research does not confirm findings on the lengthening effect for the optimal rotation period due to the inclusion of CS benefits (see also Stainback and Alavalapati, 2002). In nearly all cases, the maximized LEV_j occurs in year 8 of a considered rotation period of 40 years. That indicates first, that the CS benefits are not strong enough to increase the optimal rotation period as expected. Second, it suggests a harvest age that from a non-economic viewpoint is too early and not concordant with the common harvest age in the region of about 25 years. However, it has to be emphasized that the results indicate only the financial optimal harvest age and therefore have to be treated as such. Potentially, the results concerning harvest age can be caused by the financial structure of the representative plantation or by the volumes used.

The sensitivity analysis carried out also did not lead to different findings on the early optimal rotation age but confirmed what theory suggests; that the value of the joint forestland depends on the volume function, the value for timber and non- timber (i.e. carbon revenues), and the discount rate. Further, the sensitivity analysis showed to what extent the market value of the land has an impact on profitability. The LEV_J responded to the simulated change of each of the factors as expected which leads to the conclusion that the overall profitability model applied in theory is suitable to determine the profitability of forest activities. However, the determined early optimal financial rotation age may require further revision to support the findings of the LEV_J.

Considering the results from a broader perspective, the research supports the emphasis made on the link between mitigation and adaptation within a new framework of concepts. It shows that forestry projects (i.e. plantation projects) function as sinks and thus mitigate. At the same time, it also discloses the necessity to adapt since climate change, as suggested by the results, adversely affects forest productivity. Adaptation measures that include, for instance, alterations of management regimes, or land use changes are possible options to the landholders. However, before appropriate measures can be taken, a further, more thorough assessment needs to be carried out. This suggests that further research is needed. The approach of this research intended to show what is recognized increasingly at the policy level and is in line with research from e.g. Verchot et al. (2005), Rita et al. (2007), Yin et al. (2007), and Cacho et al. (2008): carbon forest projects need to be viewed as embedded in a wider reality. This reality does not only connect adaptation to mitigation, but also considers sustainable development, income generation to alleviate poverty, and community development. The overall result of the research supports that additional income generation is of benefit to landholders by increasing the forest activity's profitability. As already discussed, due to the small benefits with present carbon prices, landholders will not base their decision on whether to carry out forestry activities based on CS benefits. Therefore, carbon prices need to be high enough to make an activity including CS services worthwhile. Moreover, the decrease in volume leads to great adverse effects that need to be either compensated for, or else landholders will need to adapt by possibly switching to other activities. These interlinked issues raise several points of discussion that are briefly introduced in the following.

First, the analysis shows that, despite the mitigation potential, the activities in many cases are not profitable for the landholders under future climate regimes. The question is whether the approach of mitigating climate change by sustaining forest activities is a desired option, bearing in mind that these activities may become unprofitable under future climate already when only timber sales are considered. Thus, can climate change mitigation offset sufficient future damage to justify economically unprofitable projects for the sake of carbon sequestration? This relates to a further question of what the true costs of climate change are in order to sufficiently provide for carbon sequestration as a global public good to mitigate climate change. Furthermore, adaptation strategies need to be assessed and implemented. If the projects are sustained by paying carbon prices high enough, it is debatable whether landholders will participate. Are they nevertheless going to adapt to volume changes, for instance by improving their management practices, or will high carbon prices also prevent them from switching to other activities, for instance agriculture or tourism, that in turn capture and store less carbon?

Second, additional income generation due to carbon forestry projects implies that access to carbon markets needs to be guaranteed. This thesis did not investigate the viability of carbon market for forest plantations. The voluntary markets are considered a possible option as regulatory markets involve, for instance, high transaction costs. Although the voluntary market allows individuals to trade carbon offsets, landholders may nevertheless face access problems, leaving them with bigger companies or national agencies as actors to undertake the negotiations. Although programmes by the national agency FONAFIFO in Costa Rica are substantial and an increasing number of projects focus on carbon sequestration as an ecosystem benefit, it may be possible that very few landholders can participate due to these access problems. The discussion raises the question of how realistic the possibility is for the landholders in Costa Rica to actually access and obtain carbon credits.

The third and last point to be made is that carbon forestry projects without doubt constitute a cost-effective measure to mitigate climate change that needs to be more fully exploited. However, it is critical to view carbon sequestration projects, and thus also forest CS projects, as short term measures that support mitigation. However, they cannot be the ultimate measures in terms of mitigation on the way to combat climate change, but part of a portfolio that, for instance, considers a substantial transformation of the transportation and energy sector.

8.2 Conclusions

The presented site and species specific research on teak plantations located on the Pacific Coast of Costa Rica suggests that climate change affects the profitability of carbon credit sales. Specifically, the results show that climate change in terms of changing temperature and precipitation has an adverse effect on tree productivity. The calibrated climate- yield model, that estimates volume based on age and climate factors, results in substantial decreases in volume when projections of climate change scenarios for Costa Rica are applied to historic climate data. This emphasizes the joint negative effect of temperature and precipitation on tree volume considering climate projections. However, the analysis suggests that the impacts vary between regions depending on present climatic patterns and the projections made. This supports the detected individual effects of temperature and precipitation. Individually, it can be concluded that temperature with its projected homogenous increase in mean annual temperature in all regions has negative impacts, whereas a projected increase in precipitation as in the Central Pacific may counteract the adverse impact of temperature to some extent. In that way, the research implies, based on the climate- yield model, that the drier North Pacific region- under local and global climate scenarios- will suffer substantially greater losses in tree volume than the Central Pacific.

Further, the research confirms that the effects of future climate on total tree volume translate into consequences for the volume of timber and carbon sequestration- both subject of the profitability analysis. This profitability analysis, which employs the Joint Land Expectation Value as a criterion, provides the following results: (i) in line with the decreasing volume pattern, the overall profitability of forest projects based exclusively on timber, or timber and CS benefits (with or without PES in either case) declines; (ii) the inclusion of carbon sequestration benefits increases the profitability of the forest project when compared to solely considering timber benefits; and (iii) as the overall profitability decreases with future volume scenarios, also the profitability of carbon credit sales declines substantially. Despite the decrease in profitability, the research contributes to the ensuing conclusions regarding the profitability of carbon credit sales on (i) where adverse impacts may occur least for forest projects that take into account CS benefits; and on (ii) that the inclusion of CS benefits always compensates, even if only to a little extent, for adverse climate change impacts; but that however; (iii) current carbon prices are not high enough to counteract adverse climate change impacts on the profitability of forest projects. The study indicates that for the worst affected region in future only a carbon price of about 330 US $ per t CO2e would remedy the situation and make the project slightly profitable.

On the overall for the research, it can be concluded that the effects of climate change on tree productivity translate into a decline in profitability of the forest project as such and accordingly, also in profitability when carbon sequestration benefits in terms of carbon credits are considered.

8.3   Recommendations

The recommendations for further research and for policy are addressed in the following. The methodological approach of an integrated assessment applied in the research is meant to assist future site and species specific research that links ecological and economic aspects of climate change. The methods used in particular for the calibration of the climate- yield model can be further refined in future research. Despite that the overall aim was to analyse the impact of climate change on tree productivity, climate change is not fully accounted for in the model as it only refers to changes in temperature and precipitation, but leaves out the joint effect of these variables with CO_2. Furthermore, also alterations in patterns of climate variability or intensity or frequency would need to be considered, leaving possible starting points for future research. Furthermore, future interdisciplinary research can appropriately account for other growth factors than climate, as these could not have been taken into account in this research. Another follow up point can consist, for example, in the refinement of data on carbon stock potentials of teak and relevant tropical species. Regarding further possible steps in the economic analysis, future research can integrate the impact of non constant timber and carbon prices in the provided framework, and analyse the effects of carbon specific discount rates. In addition, other studies can provide the relevant information on accessibility of landholders to the voluntary carbon markets or other carbon offset trading schemes in future.

Recommendations for policy range from broad recommendations for the international level regarding climate change impact assessment and integration into the current framework, to more specific recommendations for the national level that concern, for instance, improved access to carbon projects. The integrated site and species specific research of this research links ecological and economic aspects. It aims at assessing the impact of climate change on natural resources, on the mitigation potential of these resources, as well as on the consequences for the income of the resources' property right holders. These assessments serve to identify necessary adaptation strategies with respect to, for instance, alternative incomes, resource management, and also, the development of alternative mitigation strategies.

International climate policy needs to facilitate the implementation of these assessments, the synthesization of information and the establishment of an accessible and transparent knowledge base. Next, the suggested regional difference in the effects of climate change on carbon sequestration and its profitability show the need to further integrate adaptation with mitigation, and at the same time development. As climate change may affect the goods and services that forest provide with variance between regions, assessment is needed for adaptation measures to ensure the delivery of carbon sequestration to mitigate and to provide income to the landholders to alleviate poverty.

On national policy level in specific, access to carbon sequestration programmes needs to be facilitated for eligible forest projects; funds need to be made available for research institutes and universities to carry out the linked ecological-economic assessments; and appropriate dissemination scheme of the information on climate change impact need to be in place.

References

Alig, R. J., D. Adams, L. Joyce and B. Sohngen (2004). 'Climate Change Impacts and Adaptation in Forestry: Responses by Trees and Markets', American Agricultural Economics Association, 19 (3).

Amézquita, M. C., E. Murgueitio R, C. A. Cuartas and M. E. Gómez (without year). Almacenamiento de carbono en ecosistemas terrestres para mitigar el cambio climático global. CATIE, Turrialba (Costa Rica), CIAT, Cali (Columbia), Wageningen University, Wageningen (Netherlands). Universidad de la Amazonia, Caquetá (Columbia): Florencia (Columbia).

Antle, J. M., J. J. Stoorvogel and R. O. Valdivia (2007). 'Assessing the economic impacts of agricultural carbon sequestration: terraces and agroforestry in the Peruvian Andes', Agriculture, Ecosystems and Environment, 122 (4): 435-445.

Argüello, R., B. Locatelli, G. Navarro, M. Piedra and Z. Salinas (2007). 'Potencial del Mecanismo de Desarrollo Limpio en las Plantaciones Forestales de Panama', Tierra Tropical, 3 (1): 27-36.

Aune, J. B., A. T. Alemu and K. P. Gautam (2005). 'Carbon sequestration in rural communities: Is it worth the effort?' Journal of Sustainable Forestry, 21 (1): 69-79.

Avery, T. E. and H. E. Burkhart (2002). Forest measurements, Ellefson, P. V. (ed.): McGraw-Hill Series in Forest Resources. 5th Edition. Mcgraw-Hill: Boston.

BCCR (2008a). Tipo cambio de compra y de venta del dólar de los Estados Unidos de América. Available at: http://indicadoreseconomicos.bccr.fi.cr/indicadoreseconomicos/Cuadros/frmVerCatCuadro.aspx?Idioma=1&CodCuadro=400 (Accessed on: 01-09-08).

BCCR (2008b). Indice de precios al productor industrial con combustible (IPPI). Available at: http://indicadoreseconomicos.bccr.fi.cr/indicadoreseconomicos/Cuadros/frmVerCatCuadro.aspx?idioma=1&CodCuadro=%20599 (Accessed on: 22-10-2008).

BCCR (2008c). Tasa de interés activa promedio del Sistema Financiero para préstamos en moneda nacional. Available at: http://indicadoreseconomicos.bccr.fi.cr/indicadoreseconomicos/Cuadros/frmVerCatCuadro.aspx?idioma=1&CodCuadro=%20614 (Accessed on: 22-10-2008).

Bebarta, K. C. (1999). Teak. Ecology, Silviculture, Management and Profitability. International Book Distributors: Dehra Dun (India).

Behan, J., K. McQuinn and M. J. Roche (2006). 'Rural land use: traditional agriculture or forestry?', Land Economics, 82 (1): 112-123.

Benavides, H. A. and A. B. Rodríguez (2006). La madera en Costa Rica. Situación Actual y Perspectivas. ONF and FONAFIFO. Available at: http://www.oficinaforestalcr.org/media_files/download/MADERAENCOSTARICA,SIT UACIONACTUALYPERSPECTIVAS,2006.pdf (Accessed on: 15-05-2008).

Bhat, K. M., P. K. Thulasidas and K. H. Hussain (2007). A handbook of lesser known timbers, In: KFRI Research Report No. 304. Kerala Forest Research Institute: Peechi, Kerala (India). Available at: http://teaknet.org/images/HandBook%20sample%20pages.pdf (Accessed on: 11-05-2009).

Binkley, C. S., M. J. Apps, R. K. Dixon, P. E. Kauppi and L. O. Nilsson (1997). 'Sequestering carbon in natural forests', Critical Reviews in Environmental Science and Technology, 27: S23-S45.

Bishop, J. T. (1998). The Economics of Non-Timber Forest Benefits: An Overview, In: Environmental Economics Programme. GK 98-01. IIED.

Boisvenue, C. and S. W. Running (2006). 'Impacts of climate change on natural forest productivity – evidence since the middle of the 20th century', Global Change Biology, (12): 862–882.

Boyland, M. (2006). 'The economics of using forests to increase carbon storage', Canadian Journal of Forest Research, 36 (9): 2223-2234.

Brack, C. and G. Wood (1998). Tree Growth and Increment. Australian National University: Canberra (Australia). Available at: http://fennerschool-associated.anu.edu.au//mensuration/BrackandWood1998/INDEX.HTM (Accessed on: 15-03-2009).

Brown, S., C. A. S. Hall, W. Knabe, J. Raich, M. C. Trexler and P. Woomer (1993). 'Tropical forests: Their past, present, and potential future role in the terrestrial carbon budget', Water, Air, and Soil Pollution, 70 (1-4): 71-94.

Cacho, O., R. Hean, K. Ginoga, R. Wise, D. Djaenudin, M. Lugina, Y. Wulan, Subarudi, B. Lusiana, M. v. Noordwijk and N. Khasanah (2008). Economic potential of land-use change and forestry for carbon sequestration and poverty reduction. ACIAR: ACIAR Technical Reports Series, 68: Canberra (Australia). Available at: http://www.aciar.gov.au/publication/TR68 (Accessed on: 15-11-2009).

Cacho, O. J., R. M. Wise and K. G. MacDicken (2004). 'Carbon monitoring costs and their effect on incentives to sequester carbon through forestry', Mitigation and Adaptation Strategies for Global Change, 9 (3): 273-293.

Calish, S., R. D. Fight and D. E. Teeguarden (1978). 'How Do Nontimber Values Affect Douglas-fir Rotations?', Journal of Forestry: 217-221.

Cannell, M. G. R. (1996). 'Forests as carbon sinks mitigating the greenhouse effect', Commonwealth Forestry Review, 75 (1): 92-99.

CATIE (2005). Ejemplo: calculó del VET de plantaciones. Curso economía forestal. CATIE, Turrialba, Costa Rica.

Cervi, A. P. (2006). Zonificación edafoclimática de aptitud para especies forestales en escenarios de cambio climático: une Studio de caso de Costa Rica. CATIE and University of São Paulo: Internship report within the TroFCCA Project (Tropical Forests and Climate Change Adaptation): Turrialba (Costa Rica), São Paulo (Brasil).

Chambers, J. Q. and W. L. Silver (2004). 'Some aspects of ecophysiological and biogeochemical responses of tropical forests to atmospheric change', Philosophical Transactions of the Royal Society B: Biological Sciences, 359 (1443): 463-476.

Chaves S., E. and W. Fonseca G. (2003). 'Ensayos de aclareo y crecimiento en plantaciones de teca (Tectona grandis L.f.) en la Península de Nicoya, Costa Rica.' In: Plantaciones de Teca (Tectona grandis). Posibilidades y perspectivas para su desarrollo, Heredia (Costa Rica), 26-28 November 2003. INISEFOR, UNA Available at: http://www.una.ac.cr/inis/tecatema.htm (Accessed on: 15-09-2008).

Chladna, Z. (2007). 'Determination of optimal rotation period under stochastic wood and carbon prices', Forest Policy and Economics, 9 (8): 1031-1045.

Chomitz, K. M., E. Brenes and L. Constantino (1999). 'Financing environmental services: the Costa Rican experience and its implications', The Science of The Total Environment, 240 (1-3): 157-169.

Clark, D. A., S. C. Piper, C. D. Keeling and D. B. Clark (2003). Tropical rain forest tree growth and atmospheric carbon dynamics linked to interannual temperature variation during 1984–2000. Summary. Available at: http://www.pnas.org/content/100/10/5852.full.pdf (Accessed on: 10-07-2008).

Clutter, J. L., J. C. Fortson, L. V. Pienaar, G. H. Brister and R. L. Bailey (1983). Timber management: a quantitative approach. Wiley: New York.

Cosbey, A., J.-E. Parry, J. Browne, Y. Dinesh Babu, P. Bhandari, J. Drexhage and D. Murphy (2005). Realizing the Development Dividend: Making the CDM Work for Developing Countries. IISD: Phase 1 Report – Prepublication Version: Winnipeg, Manitoba (Canada). Available at: http://www.iisd.org/pdf/2005/climate_realizing_dividend.pdf (Accessed on: 15-11-2008).

Cubero, J. A. and S. R. Rojas (1999). Fijación de carbono en plantaciones de melina (Gmelina arborea Roxb.), teca (Tectona grandis L.f:) y pochote (Bombacopsis quinata Jacq.) en los cantones de Hojancha y Nicoya, Guanacaste, Costa Rica. Available at: http://cglobal.imn.ac.cr/Pdf/mitigacion/Estudio%20sobre%20Fijacion%20de%20Carbono%20en%20Plantaciones.pdf (Accessed on: 14-07-2008).

Diaz-Balteiro, L. and L. C. E. Rodriguez (2006). 'Optimal rotations on Eucalyptus plantations including carbon sequestration - A comparison of results in Brazil and Spain', Forest Ecology and Management, 229 (1-3): 247-258.

Dixon, R. K. (1997). 'Silvicultural options to conserve and sequester carbon in forest systems: Preliminary economic assessment', Critical Reviews in Environmental Science and Technology, 27: S139-S149.

Easterling, W. and M. Apps (2005). "Assessing the consequences of climate change for food and forest resources: a view from the IPCC." In: Increasing climate variability and change. Reducing the vulnerability of agriculture and forestry. Eds. Salinger, J., M. V. K. Sivakumar and R. P. Motha. Springer. Dordrecht (Netherlands). Electronic book. Available at: http://books.google.nl/books?id=ojwLpBZfzAYC&pg=PA165&lpg=PA165&dq=Assessing+the+Consequences+of+Climate+Change+for+Food+and+forest+Resources:+A+View+from+the+IPCC&source=bl&ots=EJGe4bhlRw&sig=aS0srxg9Q3XV4o20YtIca94b9kE&hl=nl&ei=PqpwSpmZDJbSjAfkwaSeBQ&sa=X&oi=book_result&ct=result&resnum=7 (Accessed on: 10-03-2009).

Easterling, W. E., P. K. Aggarwal, P. Batima, K. M. Brander, L. Erda, S. M. Howden, A. Kirilenko, J. Morton, J.-F. Soussana, J. Schmidhuber and F. N. Tubiello (2007). "Food, fibre and forest products." In: Climate Change 2007: Impacts, Adaptation and Vulnerability. Contribution of Working Group II to the Fourth Assessment Report of the Intergovernmental Panel on Climate Change. Eds. Parry, M. L., O. F. Canziani, J. P. Palutikof, P. J. Van der Linden and C. E. Hanson. Cambridge University Press. Cambridge (UK).

Faustmann, M. (1849). On the determination of the value which forest land and imma-
ture stands pose for forestry, In: Gane, M. (ed.), Martin Faustmann and the Evolu-
tion of Discounted Cash Flow. Oxford Institute: Oxford.

Fearnside, P. M. (2004). 'Are climate change impacts already affecting tropical forest
biomass?', Global Environmental Change, 14: 299–302.

FONAFIFO (2007). Acerca del FONAFIFO. Available at:
http://www.fonafifo.com/paginas_espanol/fonafifo/e_fo_acerca.htm (Accessed on:
12-09-2008).

FONAFIFO (2008). Oferta de Proyectos de "Absorción de CO2 a través de actividades de
aforestación /reforestación dentro del Mecanismo de Desarrollo Limpio",In:
FONAFIFO - 2006 and Carbon Sequestration in Small and Medium Farms in the
Brunca Region, Costa Rica (CoopeAgri Project). Available at:
http://www.fonafifo.com/paginas_espanol/noticias/e_nt_noti001.htm (Accessed
on: 13-03-2008).

Garcia-Gonzalo, J., H. Peltola, E. Bricenño-Elizondo and S. Kellomäki (2007). 'Effects of
climate change and management on timber yield in boreal forests, with economic
implications: A case study', Ecological Modelling, 209 (2-4): 220-234.

Grainger, A. (1997). 'Compensating for opportunity costs in forest-based global climate
change mitigation', Critical Reviews in Environmental Science and Technology, 27:
S163-S176.

Gregory, G. R. (1987). Resource economics for foresters. John Wiley & Sons: New York.

Gutierrez, V. H., M. Zapata, C. Sierra, W. Laguado and A. Santacruz (2006). 'Maximizing
the profitability of forestry projects under the Clean Development Mechanism using
a forest management optimization model', Forest Ecology and Management, 226
(1-3): 341-350.

Hamilton, K., M. Sjardin, T. Marcello and G. Xu (2008). Forging a Frontier: State of the
Voluntary Carbon Markets 2008. Ecosystem Marketplace & New Carbon Finance.

Hoen, H. F. and B. Solberg (1997). 'CO2-Taxing, Timber Rotations, and Market Implications', Critical Reviews in Environmental Science and Technology, 27 (Special Issue):
S151-S162.

Hooda, N. and V. R. S. Rawat (2006). 'Role of bio-energy plantations for carbon-dioxide
mitigation with special reference to India', Mitigation and Adaptation Strategies for
Global Change, 11 (2): 445-467.

Huang, C. H. and G. D. Kronrad (2001). 'The cost of sequestering carbon on private forest lands', Forest Policy and Economics, 2 (2): 133-142.

Huang, C. H. and G. D. Kronrad (2006). 'The effect of carbon revenues on the rotation and profitability of loblolly pine plantations in East Texas', Southern Journal of Applied Forestry, 30 (1): 21-29.

IFAM (1985). Costa Rica- provincias y cantones, In: Atlas Cantonal de Costa Rica. Preparado por el Instituto de Fomento y Asesoría Municipal en colaboración con el Instituto Geográfico Nacional de Costa Rica. Edición provisional 1985. Available at: http://ccp.ucr.ac.cr/bvp/mapoteca/CostaRica/generales/atlas_cantonal_1984/02-Provincias_Cantones-CR.pdf (Accessed on: 03-05-2009).

IISD (2008). Summary of the fourteenth Conference of the parties to the UN Framework Convention and the fourth Meeting of the Parties to the Kyoto Protocol: 1-12 December 2008. Available at: http://www.iisd.ca/download/pdf/enb12395e.pdf (Accessed on: 15-12-2008).

IMN (2009). Regional maps of the Pacific Coast in Costa Rica including climate stations and teak plantations. Ed. Araya, C.

IMN (without year). Datos meteorológicos de varias estaciones climáticas In: Tables for climate stations Nicoya (Nicoya.xls), Paquera (Paquera-Cobano.xls), Santa Cruz (St. Cruz.xls), Damas (Damas.xls), and Pocares (lluvia- POCARES CAMBIO CLIMATICO.xls). Ed. Retana, J. A.

INEC (2009). Sobre Costa Rica. Available at: http://www.inec.go.cr/ (Accessed on: 09-01-09).

INISEFOR (2006). GPS coordinates, In: GpsTeca.xls. Coordinates of locations Santa Cruz, Nicoya 1, Nicoya 2, Norman Quieros in Rio Negro, Bosque 3 in Puerto Carrillo, Cabuya, and Cobano. Eds. Mora, F. and H. Toruño.

INISEFOR (without year. a). Análisis fustal de un árbol de Tectona grandis (Teca). Vertiente Pacifica de Costa Rica., In: Measurement tables for locations Santa Cruz (NICOYVG4.xls, STCRPD2.xls), Nicoya 1 (NICOYVG5.xls, NICOYVG3.xls), Nicoya 2 (NICOYPG2), Finca Valeria (VALERIA.xls), Finca Tigre (TIGRE.xls), Finca Rios (RIOSD19.xls, RIOST22.xls, RIOSD20.xls, RIOST17.xls) within period 1952-1992. Ed. Mora, F.

INISEFOR (without year. b). Datos promedios de las parcelas de teca en Cabuya, Bosque 2, Cobano y Rio Negro, In: Measurement tables for locations Cabuya, Bosque 3, Cobano (tecapro08.xls) and Rio Negro (norquiedadpro.xls) within period 1984-2005. Ed. Chaves, E.

IPCC (2003). "LUCF Sector Good Practice Guidance. Appendix 3a.1. Biomass Default Tables for Section 3.2 Forest Land- Harvested wood products: Basis for future methodological development. Table 3a.1.3." In: IPCC Good Practice Guidance for Land Use, Land-Use Change and Forestry. National Greenhouse Gas Inventories Programme. Available at: http://www.ipcc-nggip.iges.or.jp/public/gpglulucf/gpglulucf_contents.html (Accessed on: 11-05-2009).

IPCC (2006). "Volume 4- Agriculture, Forestry and Other Land Use. Chapter 4: Forest Land." In: 2006 IPCC Guidelines for National Greenhouse Gas Inventories. Prepared by the National Greenhouse Gas Inventories Programme. Eds. Eggleston, H. S., L. Buendia, K. Miwa, T. Ngara and K. Tanabe. Institute for Global Environmental Strategies (IGES) on behalf of the IPCC. Hayama (Japan).

IPCC (2007). Climate Change 2007: Synthesis Report. Contribution of Working Groups I, II and III to the Fourth Assessment Report of the Intergovernmental Panel on Climate Change: Geneva (Switzerland).

Jong, B. H. J. d., G. Montoya-Gomez, K. Nelson, L. Soto-Pinto, J. Taylor and R. Tipper (1995). 'Community forest management and carbon sequestration: a feasibility study from Chiapas, Mexico', Interciencia, 20 (6): 409-416.

Kellomäki, S., T. Karjalainen and H. Väisänen (1997). 'More timber from boreal forests under changing climate?' Forest Ecology and Management, 94 (1-3): 195-208.

Keogh, R. M. (2002). 'TEAK 21: a support mechanism for high-grade tropical hardwoods', International Forestry Review, 4 (3).

Keogh, R. M. (2005). Carbon models and tables for teak (Tectona grandis Linn f.); Central America and The Carribean. Coillte consult. International Teak Unit. Available at: http://www.coillte.ie/fileadmin/templates/pdfs/Carbon_and_Volume_Tables_for_Teak_jan_04-doc.pdf (Accessed on: 10-11-2008).

Kirby, K. R. and C. Potvin (2007). 'Variation in carbon storage among tree species: Implications for the management of a small-scale carbon sink project', Forest Ecology and Management, 246 (2-3): 208-221.

Klemperer, W. D. (1996). Forest Resource Economics and Finance, Ellefson, P. V. (ed.): McGraw-Hill Series in Forest Resources. McGraw-Hill, Inc.: New York.

Kollmuss, A., M. Lazarus, C. Lee and C. Polycarp (2008). A Review of Offset Programs: Trading Systems, Funds, Protocols, Standards and Retailers. Stockholm Environment Institute US: SEI Research Report: Boston (US). Available at: http://www.sei.se/publications.html?task=view&catid=2&id=837 (Accessed on: 10-01-2009).

Kraenzel, M., A. Castillo, T. Moore and C. Potvin (2003). 'Carbon storage of harvest-age teak (Tectona grandis) plantations, Panama', Forest Ecology and Management, 173 (1-3): 213-225.

Lal, R. (2005). 'Soil Carbon Sequestration in Natural and Managed Tropical Forest Eco-systems', Journal of Sustainable Forestry, Vol. 21 (No. 1): pp. 1-30.

Lewis-Beck, M. S., A. Bryman and T. F. Liao (2004). The SAGE encyclopaedia of social science research methods, (2), Thousand Oaks, Sage Publications: California. Electronic Book. Available at: http://books.google.nl/books?id=eYhW4bbsdBYC&printsec=frontcover (Accessed on: 14-07-09).

Ley, E. and R. A. Sedjo (1997a). 'Carbon sequestration and tree plantations: A case study in Argentina', Critical Reviews in Environmental Science and Technology, 27: S185-S192.

Ley, E. and R. A. Sedjo (1997b). 'Optimal subsidies for carbon: Cost-effectiveness and distributional considerations', Critical Reviews in Environmental Science and Technology, 27: S177-S184.

Li, N., Y. Gong and S. Zhang (2006). 'Forestry carbon sequestration projects in China - a synergized strategy of mitigation, adaptation and sustainable development', World Forestry Research, 19 (3): 1-5.

Lin, J., K. J. Lee and Y. Lin (1999). 'A study on carbon sinking effect and adaptation cost of Cryptomeria japonica', Journal of the Experimental Forest of National Taiwan University, 13 (1): 51-60.

Lindner, M., F. W. Badeck, P. Bartelheimer, S. Bonk, W. Cramer, M. Dieter, H. Döbbeler, J. Dursky, C. Duschi, M. Fabrika, D. Frömdling, E. Gundermann, P. Hennig, W. Hölzer, P. Lasch, B. Leischner, M. Liesebach, A. Pommerening, M. Pott, H. Pretzsch, W. Schlott, F. Scholtz, H. Spellmann, F. Suckow and M. Suda (2002a). 'Integrating forest growth dynamics, forest economics and decision making to assess the sensitivity of the German Forest sector to climate change', Integration von Waldentwicklungsdynamik, Forstökonomie und Entscheidungsverhalten in Forstbetrieben zur Beurteilung der Gefährdung der Deutschen Forstwirtschaft durch den Klimawandel, 121 (SUPPLEMENT 1): 191-208.

Lindner, M. and W. Cramer (2002). 'German Forest Sector under Global Change: An interdisciplinary impact assessment', Wälder und Forstwirtschaft Deutschlands im globalen Wandel: Eine interdisziplinäre Wirkungsanalyse, 121 (SUPPLEMENT 1): 3-17.

Lindner, M., B. Sohngen, L. A. Joyce, D. T. Price, P. Y. Bernier and T. Karjalainen (2002b). 'Integrated forestry assessments for climate change impacts', Forest Ecology and Management, 162 (1): 117-136.

Locatelli and Pedroni (2003, p. 80). 'Accounting methods for carbon credits: impacts on the minimum size of CDM forestry projects.' Global Change Group, CATIE, Turrialba.
.

Long, S. J. and J. Freese (2006). Regression Models for Categorial Dependent Variables Using Stata. 2nd Edition. Stata Press: Texas.

Marland, G., B. Schlamadinger and P. Leiby (1997). 'Forest/biomass based mitigation strategies: Does the timing of carbon reductions matter?' Critical Reviews in Environmental Science and Technology, 27: S213-S226.

Masera, O., M. R. Bellon and G. Segura (1997). 'Forestry options for sequestering carbon in Mexico: Comparative economic analysis of three case studies', Critical Reviews in Environmental Science and Technology, 27: S227-S244.

McKenzie, T. A. (2004). Estudio de tendencias y perspectivas del Sector Forestal en América Latina, In: Documento de Trabajo. Informe Nacional de Costa Rica. FAO: San José (Costa Rica). Available at: http://www.fao.org/docrep/007/j3397s/j3397s11.htm (Accessed on: 6.1.2008).

Mena, M. (without year). Clima de Costa Rica. IMN: San Jose. Available at: http://www.imn.ac.cr/educacion/CLIMA%20DE%20COSTA%20RICA.html (Accessed on: 09-01-2009).

MINAE (2008). Decreto Ejecutivo 2008. Articulo 2b, (Nº 34371-MINAE). Available at: http://www.fonafifo.com/paginas_espanol/servicios_ambientales/sa_decreManua.htm (Accessed on: 23-10-2008).

MINAE and IMN (2008). Proyección del clima futuro en Costa Rica- Primer avance. Proyecto Segunda Comunicación sobre Cambio Climático: San José (Costa Rica).

MINAE and PNDF (2002). El Éxito Forestal de Costa Rica- En cinco casos. San José (Costa Rica).

Mohamed, M. A. A., I. S. Babiker, Z. M. Chen, K. Ikeda, K. Ohta and K. Kato (2004). 'The role of climate variability in the inter-annual variation of terrestrial net primary production (NPP)', Science of the Total Environment, 332 (1-3): 123-137.

Mora, F. and V. Meza (2003). 'Comparación del crecimiento en altura de la Teca (Tectona grandis) en Costa Rica con otros trabajos previos y con otras regiones del mundo' In: Plantaciones de Teca (Tectona grandis). Posibilidades y perspectivas para su desarrollo, Heredia (Costa Rica), 26-28 November 2003. INISEFOR, UNA. Available at: http://www.una.ac.cr/inis/tecatema.htm (Accessed on: 15-09-2008).

Murdiyarso, D., H. Herawati and H. Iskandar (2005). Carbon sequestration and sustainable livelihoods: a workshop synthesis. CIFOR: Bogor Barat (Indonesia). Available at: http://www.cifor.cgiar.org/Publications/Detail?pid=1757 (Accessed on: 15-11-2008).

Nagata, S. (2004). 'Market-based instruments for watershed protection—what do we know? ', In: Proceedings of the Workshop Forests for Poverty Reduction: Opportunities with Clean Development Mechanism, Environmental Services and Biodiversity, Seoul (Korea), 27–29 August 2003. RAP Publication 2004/22. Eds. H.C. Sim, S. Appanah and Y.C. Youn. FAO, Bangkok.

Navarro, G. A. (2003a). On 189 Years of Confusing Debates over the König-Faustmann Formula. Albert-Ludwigs-Universität: Freiburg.

Navarro, G. A. (2003b). 'Diseño y Análisis Microeconómico de los Mecanismos Monetarios de Fomento a las Plantaciones Forestales en Costa Rica ' In: Jornada de reforestación en Costa Rica. La reforestación costarricense: hacia la transformación hacia mercados abiertos Heredia (Costa Rica), 19-20 Junio 2003. INISEFOR, UNA. Available at: http://www.una.ac.cr/inis/refor.htm (Accessed on: 15-09-2008).

Noordwijk, M. v., D. A. Suyamto, B. Lusiana, A. Ekadinata and K. Hairiah (2008). 'Facilitating agroforestation of landscapes for sustainable benefits: tradeoffs between carbon stocks and local development benefits in Indonesia according to the FALLOW model', Agriculture, Ecosystems and Environment, 126 (1/2): 98-112.

Nuutinen, T., J. Matala, H. Hirvela, K. Härkönen, H. Peltola, H. Väisänen and S. Kellomäki (2006). 'Regionally optimized forest management under changing climate', Climatic Change, 79 (3-4): 315-333.

Oderwald, R. G. and W. A. Duerr (1990). 'König-Faustmannism: A Critique. Discussion Paper', Forest Science, 36 (1): 169-174.

ONF (2004). Costa Rica Forestal- Boletín Informativo de la Oficina Nacional Forestal. Enero - Febrero 2004. Available at: http://www.oficinaforestalcr.org/media_files/download/BoletinOficialONFCostaRicaForestalN%C2%BA01-2004.pdf (Accessed on: 11-07-2008).

Ortiz M., E. and J. Kellenberg (without year). Program of Payments for Ecological Services in Costa Rica. Instituto Tecnológico de Costa Rica; Regional Unit for Technical Assistance and Sr. Natural Resources Economist – The World Bank. Available at: http://ecosystemmarketplace.com/documents/cms_documents/lr_ortiz_kellenberg _ext.1.pdf (Accessed on: 10-02-2009).

Ortiz, R. and M. Kanninen (1999). 'Evaluación económica del servicio de sumidero de carbono en diferentes ecosistemas forestales. Logros de la investigación para el nuevo milenio. En: Línea 5: Valoración y análisis socio- económico de políticas de sistemas de manejo y de bienes y servicios de ecosistemas tropicales. En: Actas de la IV Semana Científica' In: 4. Semana Científica, Turrialba (Costa Rica), 6-9 April 1999. CATIE: Programa de Investigación. Serie Técnica. Reuniones Técnicas (CATIE). No. 5.: Turrialba (Costa Rica).

Pandey, D. (1996). 'Estimating Productivity of Tropical Forest Plantations by Climatic Factors', Swedish University of Agricultural Sciences, Department of Forest Resource Management and Geomatics Umea, Report 7.

Parks, P. J., D. O. Hall, B. Kristrom, O. R. Masera, R. J. Moulton, A. J. Plantinga, J. N. Swisher and J. K. Winjum (1997). 'An economic approach to planting trees for carbon storage', Critical Reviews in Environmental Science and Technology, 27: S9-S21.

Pereira de Rezende, J. L., A. Donizette de Oliveira and L. M. Coelho Júnior (2005). Infinite planning horizon, land opportunity cost and Faustmann methodology. UFLA; Instituto de Educação Afonso Cláudio: Brasil. Available at: http://www.dcf.ufla.br/cerne/artigos/v11_n2_artigo%2001.pdf (Accessed on: 10-10-2008).

Perez-Garcia, J., L. A. Joyce, C. S. Binkley and A. D. McGuire (1997). 'Economic impacts of climatic change on the global forest sector: An integrated ecological/economic assessment', Critical Reviews in Environmental Science and Technology, 27 (Special Issue): S123-S138.

Perez, D. (2005). Stand growth scenarios for Tectona grandis plantations in Costa Rica. Faculty of Agriculture and Forestry, Department of Forest Ecology. University of Helsinki: Helsinki.

Perman, R., Y. Ma, J. McGilvray and M. Common (2003). Natural Resource and Environmental Economics. 3rd Edition. Pearson Education Limited Harlow (UK).

Phillips, G. B. (1995). 'Growth functions for teak (Tectona grandis Linn. F.) plantations in Sri Lanka', Commonwealth Forestry Review, 74 (4): 361-375.

Plantinga, A. J. (1997). 'The cost of carbon sequestration in forests: A positive analysis', Critical Reviews in Environmental Science and Technology, 27: S269-S277.

Point Carbon (2009). Carbon 2009. Emission trading coming home. Available at: http://www.pointcarbon.com/research/carbonmarketresearch/analyst/1.1083366 (Accessed on: 05-06-2009).

Reddy, S. R. C. and P. Colin (1999). 'Carbon Sequestration and Conservation of Tropical Forests Under Uncertainty', Journal of Apicultural Economics, 50 (1): 17-35.

Redondo-Brenes, A. (2005). 'Payment for Environmental Services in Costa Rica: Carbon Sequestration Estimations of Native Tree Plantations', Tropical Resources Bulletin, 24.

Reilly, J., S. Paltseva, B. Felzerb, X. Wanga, D. Kicklighterb, J. Melillob, R. Prinna, M. Sarofima, A. Sokolova and C. Wang (2007). 'Global economic effects of changes in crops, pasture, and forests due to changing climate, carbon dioxide, and ozone', Energy Policy, 35 (11): 5370–5383.

Reyes, G., S. Brown, J. Chapman and A. E. Lugo (1992). Wood densities of tropical tree species. U.S. Department of Agriculture, Forest Service New Orleans, LA (US).

Richards, K. R. (1997). 'The time value of carbon in bottom-up studies', Critical Reviews in Environmental Science and Technology, 27: S279-S292.

Rita, S., J. Xu and G. Sharma (2007). 'Traditional agroforestry in the eastern Himalayan region: land management system supporting ecosystem services', Tropical Ecology, 48 (2): 189-200.

Roshetko, J. M., R. D. Lasco and M. S. d. Los-Angeles (2007). 'Smallholder agroforestry systems for carbon storage', Mitigation and Adaptation Strategies for Global Change, 12 (2): 219-242.

Rousseeuw, P. J. and A. M. Leroy (1987). Robust regression and outlier detection, Wiley: New York. Electronic book. Available at: http://books.google.nl/books?id=woaH_73s-MwC&printsec=frontcover&source=gbs_navlinks_s (Accessed on: 16-07-2009).

Sampson, R. N. and R. A. Sedjo (1997). 'Economics of Carbon Sequestration in Forestry: An Overview', Critical Reviews in Environmental Science and Technology, 27 (Special Issue): S1-S8.

Samuelson, P. A. (1954). 'The Pure Theory of Public Expenditure', The Review of Economics and Statistics, 36 (4): 387-389. Published by: The MIT Press.

Samuelson, P. A. and W. D. Nordhaus (1995). Economics. International Edition. 15th Edition. McGraw-Hill.

Sánchez, O. (2002). 'El uso de especies nativas en proyectos de reforestación promovidos por el estado en Costa Rica' In: Especies forestales nativas. Memoria del taller- seminario, Heredia (Costa Rica), 4-5 April 2002. INISEFOR, UNA.

Sánchez, P. A. (2000). 'Linking climate change research with food security and poverty reduction in the tropics', Agriculture, Ecosystems and Environment, 82 (1/3): 371-383.

Saxe, H., M. G. R. Cannell, Ø. Johnsen, M. G. Ryan and G. Vourlitis (2001). 'Tree and forest functioning in response to global warming', New Phytologist, 149 (3): 369-400.

Schroeder, P. (1992). 'Carbon storage potential of short rotation tropical tree plantations', Forest Ecology & Management, 50 (1-2): 31-41.

Schumacher, F. X. (1939; cited in Clutter et al., 1983). 'A new growth curve and its application to timber-yield studies', Journal of Forestry, (37): 819-820.

Sedjo, R. and B. Sohngen (2000). Forestry Sequestration of CO2 and Markets for Timber. Discussion Paper 00–35. Resources for the Future: Washington (US). Available at: http://www.rff.org/documents/RFF-DP-00-35.pdf (Accessed on: 10-04-2008).

Sharma, R. A. (1993). 'Agroforestry vs. forestry for the rural poor: a socio-economic evaluation', Agroforestry Systems, 22 (13).

Shively, G. E., C. A. Zelek, D. J. Midmore and T. M. Nissen (2004). 'Carbon sequestration in a tropical landscape: An economic model to measure its incremental cost', Agroforestry Systems, 60 (3): 189-197.

Shvidenko, A. and M. Apps (2006). 'The International Boreal Forest Research Association: Understanding Boreal Forests and Forestry in a Changing World ', Mitigation and Adaptation Strategies for Global Change, 11 (1): 295.

Sohngen, B., R. Alig and B. Solberg (2007). The forest sector, climate change, and the global carbon cycle- environmental and economic implications. Ohio State University (US), US Dept. of Agr., Forest Service (US), Norwegian University of Life Sciences (Norway). Available at: http://www-agecon.ag.ohio-state.edu/people/sohngen.1/forests/Forestry_Climate_Survey_2007_v4.pdf (Accessed on: 10-04-2009).

Sohngen, B. and S. Brown (2008). 'Extending timber rotations: carbon and cost implications', Climate Policy, 8 (5): 435-451.

Sohngen, B. and R. Mendelsohn (1997). 'A dynamic model of forest carbon storage in the United States during climatic change', Critical Reviews in Environmental Science and Technology, 27: S309-S321.

Sohngen, B., R. Mendelsohn and R. Sedjo (2001). 'A Global Model of Climate Change Impacts on Timber Markets', Journal of Agricultural and Resource Economics, 26 (2): 326-343.

Sohngen, B. and R. Sedjo (1999). The Potential Role of Plantations in Future Timber Supply Ohio State University (US), Resources For the Future (US). Available at: http://www-agecon.ag.ohio-state.edu/people/sohngen.1/forests/planta~1.pdf (Accessed on:.

Solberg, B. (1997). 'Forest biomass as carbon sink - Economic value and forest management/policy implications', Critical Reviews in Environmental Science and Technology, 27: S323-S333.

Somarriba, E., H. J. Andrade, M. Segura and M. Villalobos (2008). '¿Como fijar carbono atmosférico, certificarlo y venderlo para complementar los ingresos de productores indígenas en Costa Rica?; How to fix atmospheric carbon in Bribri and Cabecar farms (Talamanca, Costa Rica), certify and sell it to bring additonal income to farmers', Agroforesteria en las Americas, (46): 81-88.

Stainback, G. A. and J. R. R. Alavalapati (2002). 'Economic analysis of slash pine forest carbon sequestration in the southern U. S', Journal of Forest Economics, 8 (2): 105-117.

Strengers, B. J., J. G. v. Minnen and B. Eickhout (2008). 'The role of carbon plantations in mitigating climate change: potentials and costs', Climatic Change, 88 (3/4): 343-366.

Swisher, J. N. (1997). 'Incremental costs of carbon storage in forestry, bioenergy and land-use', Critical Reviews in Environmental Science and Technology, 27: S335-S350.

Taiyab, N. (2005). The Market for Voluntary Carbon Offsets: a New Tool for Sustainable Development?. IIED: Gatekeeper Series 121. Available at: http://fletcher.tufts.edu/ierp/pdfs/NadaaTaiyab-Gatekeeper121.pdf (Accessed on: 05-05-2009).

Taiyab, N. (2006). Exploring the market for voluntary carbon offsets. IIED: London (UK). Available at: http://www.iied.org/pubs/pdfs/15502IIED.pdf (Accessed on: 05-05-2009).

Takimoto, A., P. K. R. Nair and J. R. R. Alavalapati (2008). 'Socioeconomic potential of carbon sequestration through agroforestry in the West African Sahel', Mitigation and Adaptation Strategies for Global Change, 13 (7): 745-761.

Tassone, V. C., J. Wesseler and F. S. Nesci (2004). 'Diverging incentives for afforestation from carbon sequestration: an economic analysis of the EU afforestation program in the south of Italy', Forest Policy and Economics, 6 (6): 567-578.

Thompson, W. A., G. C. van Kooten and I. Vertinsky (1997). 'Assessing timber and non-timber values in forestry using a general equilibrium framework', Critical Reviews in Environmental Science and Technology, 27: S351-S364.

UNDP (2008). 2007/2008 Human Development Report. Country Tables- Costa Rica. Available at: http://hdrstats.undp.org/en/countries/data_sheets/cty_ds_CRI.html (Accessed on: 09-01-2009).

UNFCCC (2009). CDM Statistics. Registered project activities by host party. Available at: http://cdm.unfccc.int/Statistics/Registration/NumOfRegisteredProjByHostPartiesPie Chart.html (Accessed on: 04-05-2009).

UNFCCC (without year). REDD - Web Platform. Background. Available at: http://unfccc.int/methods_science/redd/items/4547.php (Accessed on: 09-01-2009).

United Nations (1998a). Kyoto Protocol to the United Nations Framework Convention on Climate Change. Article 12. Available at: http://unfccc.int/resource/docs/convkp/kpeng.pdf (Accessed on: 13-09-2008).

United Nations (1998b). Kyoto Protocol to the United Nations Framework Convention on Climate Change. Article 3. Available at: http://unfccc.int/resource/docs/convkp/kpeng.pdf (Accessed on: 13-09-2008).

United Nations (2006a). Decision 16/CMP.1. Land use, land-use change and forestry, (FCCC/KP/CMP/2005/8/Add.3). Available at: http://unfccc.int/resource/docs/2005/cmp1/eng/08a03.pdf#page=3 (Accessed on: 14-09-2008).

United Nations (2006b). Decision 3/CMP.1. Modalities and procedures for a clean development mechanism as defined in Article 12 of the Kyoto Protocol. In: Report of the Conference of the Parties serving as the meeting of the Parties to the Kyoto Protocol on its first session, held at Montreal from 28 November to 10 December 2005. Addendum- Part Two: Action taken by the Conference of the Parties, (FCCC/KP/CMP/2005/8/Add.1). Available at: http://cdm.unfccc.int/Reference/COPMOP/08a01.pdf (Accessed on: 14-09-2008).

Van Kooten, G. C., A. Grainger, E. Ley, G. Marland and B. Solberg (1997). 'Conceptual issues related to carbon sequestration: Uncertainty and time', Critical Reviews in Environmental Science and Technology, 27: S65-S82.

Van Kooten, G. C. and B. Sohngen (2007). 'Economics of forest ecosystem carbon sinks: A review', International Review of Environmental and Resource Economics, 1 (3): 237-269.

Van Zyl, L. (2005). Stem form, height and volume models for teak in Tanzania. University of Stellenbosch: Stellenbosch. Available at: http://etd.sun.ac.za/jspui/bitstream/10019/1282/1/Van%20Zyl%2c%20L.pdf (Accessed on: 06-05-2009).

Varian, H. R. (2006). Intermediate Microeconomics. A Modern Approach. 7th Edition. W.W. Norton & Company: New York.

Venn, T. J. (2005). 'Financial and economic performance of long-rotation hardwood plantation investments in Queensland, Australia', Forest Policy and Economics, 7 (3): 437-454.

Verchot, L. V., J. Mackensen, S. Kandji, M. v. Noordwijk, T. Tomich, C. Ong, A. Albrecht, C. Bantilan, K. V. Anupama and C. Palm (2005). "Opportunities for linking adaptation and mitigation in agroforestry systems." In: Tropical forests and adaptation to climate change: in search of synergies Adaptation to climate change, sustainable livelihoods and biological diversity. Eds. Robledo, C., M. Kanninen and L. Pedroni. CIFOR. Bogor (Indonesia) Available at: http://www.sysecol.ethz.ch/pdfs/Jo64.pdf (Accessed on: 13-11-2008).

Vliet, O. P. R. v., A. P. C. Faaij and C. Dieperink (2003). 'Forestry projects under the clean development mechanism?' Climatic Change, 61 (1/2): 123-156.

Weck, J. (1970). 'An improved CVP-index for the delimitation of the potential productivity zones of forest lands of India.' Indian Forester, 96: 565–572.

Westfall, J. A. and R. L. Amateis (2003). 'A Model to Account for Potential Correlations between Growth of Loblolly Pine and Changing Ambient Carbon Dioxide Concentrations', Southern Journal of Applied Forestry, 27 (4): 279-284.

Wo Ching Sancho, E. (2001). 'Integrating Biodiversity into the Forestry Sector: Best Practice and Country Case Studies- Costa Rica' In: Integration of Biodiversity in National Forestry Planning Programme, Bogor (Indonesia), 13-16 August 2001. CIFOR.

Yaffee, R. A. (2002). Robust Regression Analysis: Some Popular Statistical Package Options New York University: Paper of the Statistics, Social Science, and Mapping Group: New York (US). Available at: http://www.nyu.edu/its/statistics/Docs/RobustReg2.pdf (Accessed on: 10-03-2009).

Yin, Y., W. Xu and S. Zhou (2007). 'Linking carbon sequestration science with local sustainability: an integrated assessment approach', Journal of Environmental Management, 85 (3): 711-721.

Zbinden, S. and D. R. Lee (2005). 'Paying for environmental services: an analysis of participation in Costa Rica's PSA program', World Development Oxford, 33 (2): 255-272.

Appendix A

Overview of tree plots and their respective historic mean climate conditions

	Location		Period of measurements		Tree age	Precipitation (mean over period)			Temperature (mean over period)	
Plot	Plantation site	Region	Starting year	Final year		TAP (in mm)	TAP dry (in mm)	TAP wet (in mm)	MAT max (in °C)	MAT min (in °C)
1	8	2	1954	1990	37	2901	337	2564	30.9	22.6
2	9	2	1953	1990	38	2901	337	2564	30.9	22.6
3	10	1	1953	1992	40	1811	59	1752	33.1	22.6
4	11	2	1953	1991	39	2901	337	2564	30.9	22.6
5	11	2	1953	1991	39	2901	554	2347	30.9	22.6
6	11	2	1952	1991	40	2901	554	2347	30.9	22.6
7	11	2	1953	1991	39	2901	337	2564	30.9	22.6
8	6	1	1979	1992	14	1731	66	1665	33.0	23.0
9	7	1	1974	1992	19	1989	92	1897	32.6	22.4
10	7	1	1979	1992	14	2037	92	1945	32.4	22.7
11	5	1	1973	1992	20	2036	91	1946	32.6	22.4
12	1	1	1989	2003	21	2104	142	1962	33.1	22.9
13	1	1	1989	2003	21	2104	142	1962	33.1	22.9
14	1	1	1989	2003	21	2104	142	1962	33.1	22.9
15	1	1	1989	2003	21	2104	142	1962	33.1	22.9
16	1	1	1989	2003	21	2104	142	1962	33.1	22.9
17	1	1	1989	2003	21	2104	142	1962	33.1	22.9
18	1	1	1989	2003	21	2104	142	1962	33.1	22.9
19	1	1	1989	2003	21	2104	142	1962	33.1	22.9
20	1	1	1989	2003	21	2104	142	1962	33.1	22.9
21	1	1	1989	2003	21	2104	142	1962	33.1	22.9
22	3	1	1995	2005	14	2119	106	2013	33.1	22.8
23	3	1	1995	2005	14	2119	106	2013	33.1	22.8
24	3	1	1995	2005	14	2119	106	2013	33.1	22.8
25	3	1	1995	2005	14	2119	106	2013	33.1	22.8
26	3	1	1995	2005	14	2119	106	2013	33.1	22.8
27	3	1	1995	2005	14	2119	106	2013	33.1	22.8
28	3	1	1995	2005	14	2119	106	2013	33.1	22.8
29	3	1	1995	2005	14	2119	106	2013	33.1	22.8
30	3	1	1995	2005	14	2119	106	2013	33.1	22.8
31	3	1	1995	2005	14	2119	106	2013	33.1	22.8
32	2	1	1984	2003	24	2000	122	1877	32.9	22.9
33	2	1	1984	2002	22	1997	122	1874	32.9	22.9
34	2	1	1984	2002	22	1997	122	1874	32.9	22.9
35	2	1	1984	2001	22	2017	125	1892	32.8	22.9
36	2	1	1984	2003	24	2000	122	1877	32.9	22.9
37	2	1	1984	2002	22	1997	122	1874	32.9	22.9
38	2	1	1995	2004	14	2170	130	2040	33.1	22.8
39	2	1	1984	2003	24	2000	122	1877	32.9	22.9
40	2	1	1984	2002	22	1997	122	1874	32.9	22.9

Overview of tree plots and their respective historic mean climate conditions
(continued)

Location			Period of measurements		Tree age	Precipitation (mean over period)			Temperature (mean over period)	
Plot	Plantation site	Region	Starting year	Final year		TAP (in mm)	TAP dry (in mm)	TAP wet (in mm)	MAT max (in °C)	MAT min (in °C)
41	2	1	1984	2003	24	2000	122	1877	32.9	22.9
42	2	1	1984	2002	22	1997	122	1874	32.9	22.9
43	2	1	1984	1996	17	2050	141	1909	32.7	22.8
44	4	1	1989	1999	14	2239	163	2076	33.0	23.0
45	4	1	1989	1999	14	2239	163	2076	33.0	23.0
46	4	1	1989	1999	14	2239	163	2076	33.0	23.0
47	4	1	1989	1999	14	2239	163	2076	33.0	23.0
48	4	1	1989	1999	14	2239	163	2076	33.0	23.0
49	4	1	1989	1999	14	2239	163	2076	33.0	23.0
50	4	1	1989	1999	14	2239	163	2076	33.0	23.0
51	4	1	1989	1999	14	2239	163	2076	33.0	23.0
52	4	1	1989	1999	14	2239	163	2076	33.0	23.0
53	4	1	1989	1999	14	2239	163	2076	33.0	23.0

Source: own elaborations based on INISEFOR (without year a. without year b) and IMN (without year)

Appendix B

Detailed financial structure of a representative teak plantation on the Pacific Coast with differentiation per activity for required workforce, material, and services for the entire rotation period

Year	Cost category	Activity	# of activity per year	Workforce			Material					Services					Total costs in ¢/ha	Total costs in US $/ha
				# of day's pay per activity	Total # of day's pay	Subtotal (¢/ha)	Product	Amount per ha	Unit	Costs per unit	Subtotal	Concept	Amount per ha	Unit	Costs per unit	Subtotal		
0	Investment	Equipment					Other tools	2		6,240	12,480						12,480	22.4
0	Investment	Equipment					Shovel	2		6,028	12,056						12,056	21.6
0	Investment	Equipment					Machete	4		1,783	7,132						7,132	12.8
0	Afforestation	Cleaning	1	2	3	23,873											23,873	42.8
0	Afforestation	Mowing	1	7	7	55,704											55,704	99.9
0	Afforestation	Marking of the area	1	3.5	3.5	27,852											27,852	50.0
0	Afforestation	Weed control	1	7	7	55,704											55,704	99.9
0	Afforestation	Opening of holes	1	5	5	39,789											39,789	71.4
0	Afforestation	Purchase and transport of plants	1				Plants	1111	Plants	102	112,952	Plant transport	1111	per unit	34	37,776	150,728	270.4
0	Afforestation	Distribution of plants and planting	1	5	5	39,789											39,789	71.4
		SUBTOTAL:															**425,106**	**762.7**
1	Maintenance (year 1)	Fertilization	2	3	6	47,746	NPK 10-30-10	23	45 kg bag	33,053	33,787						81,533	146.3
1	Maintenance (year 1)	Diversion channels	1	7	7	55,704											55,704	99.9
1	Maintenance (year 1)	Mowing	2	6.5	13	103,450											103,450	185.6
1	Maintenance (year 1)	Round firewalls	1	4	4	31,831											31,831	57.1
1	Maintenance (year 1)	Pest control	1	1	1	7,958	Virate'	0.25	litre	22,000	5,500						13,458	
1	Maintenance (year 1)	Visits forestry technicians	8									Visit		per visit	12,000	96,000	96,000	172.2
1	Maintenance (year 1)	Annual fixed costs	1			36,188						Telephone, Electricity		per year	10,000	10,000	46,188	82.9
		SUBTOTAL:															**428,164**	**744.1**

Detailed financial structure of a representative teak plantation on the Pacific Coast (continued)

Year	Cost category	Activity	# of activity per year	Workforce			Material					Services					Total costs in ¢/ha	Total costs in US $/ha
				# of day's pay per activity	Total # of day's pay	Subtotal (¢/ha)	Product	Amount per ha	Unit	Costs per unit	Subtotal	Concept	Amount per ha	Unit	Costs per unit	Subtotal		
2	Maintenance (year 2)	Diversion channels	2	7.5	15	119,366											119,366	214.2
2	Maintenance (year 2)	Mowing	2	6.5	13	103,450											103,450	185.6
2	Maintenance (year 2)	Fertilization	2	3	6	47,746	NPK 10-30-10	23	45 kg bag	33,053	33,787						81,533	146.3
2	Maintenance (year 2)	Pruning of suckers	1	4	4	31,831											31,831	57.1
2	Maintenance (year 2)	Round firewalls	1	4	4	31,831											31,831	57.1
2	Maintenance (year 2)	Visits forestry technicians	4									Visit		per visit	12,000	48,000	48,000	86.1
2	Maintenance (year 2)	Annual fixed costs	1			36,188						Telephone, Electricity		per year	10,000	10,000	46,188	82.9
		SUBTOTAL:															462,198	829.3
3	Maintenance (year 3)	Diversion channels	2	7.5	15	119,366											119,366	214.2
3	Maintenance (year 3)	Mowing	2	6.5	13	103,450											103,450	185.6
3	Maintenance (year 3)	Fertilization	1	3	3	23,873	NPK 10-30-10	23	45 kg bag	33,053	16,894						40,767	73.1
3	Maintenance (year 3)	Pruning of suckers	1	4	4	31,831											31,831	57.1
3	Maintenance (year 3)	Round firewalls	1	4	4	31,831											31,831	57.1
3	Maintenance (year 3)	Visits forestry technicians	4									Visit		per visit	12,000	48,000	48,000	86.1
3	Maintenance (year 3)	Annual fixed costs	1			36,188						Telephone, Electricity		per year	10,000	10,000	46,188	82.9
		SUBTOTAL:															421,432	756.1
4	Maintenance (year 4)	Diversion channels	2	7.5	15	119,366											119,366	214.2
4	Maintenance (year 4)	Mowing	2	6.5	13	103,450											103,450	185.6
4	Maintenance (year 4)	Round firewalls	1	4	4	31,831											31,831	57.1
4	Maintenance (year 4)	Visits forestry technicians	4									Visit		per visit	12,000	48,000	48,000	86.1
4	Maintenance (year 4)	Annual fixed costs	1			36,188						Telephone, Electricity		per year	10,000	10,000	46,188	82.9
		SUBTOTAL:															348,834	625.9

Detailed financial structure of a representative teak plantation on the Pacific Coast (continued)

Year	Cost category	Activity	# of activity per year	# of day's pay per activity	Total # of day's pay	Subtotal (¢/ha)	Product	Amount per ha	Unit	Costs per unit	Subtotal	Concept	Amount per ha	Unit	Costs per unit	Subtotal	Total costs in ¢/ha	Total costs in US $/ha
5	Maintenance (year 5)	Thinning 1: marking	1		1	7,958											7,958	14.3
5	Maintenance (year 5)	Thinning 1: cleaning	1		2	15,915											15,915	28.6
5	Maintenance (year 5)	Visits forestry technicians	4									Visit		per visit	12,000	48,000	48,000	86.1
5	Maintenance (year 5)	Annual fixed costs	1			36,188						Telephone, Electricity		per year	10,000	10,000	46,188	82.9
		SUBTOTAL:															**118,061**	**211.8**
10	Maintenance (year 10)	Thinning 2: marking	1	6.5	6.5	51,725											51,725	92.8
10	Maintenance (year 10)	Thinning 2: cleaning	1		3	23,873											23,873	42.8
10	Maintenance (year 10)	Annual fixed costs	1			36,188						Telephone, Electricity		per year	10,000	10,000	46,188	82.9
		SUBTOTAL:															**121,786**	**218.5**
15	Maintenance (year 15)	Thinning 3: marking	1		1	7,958											7,958	14.3
15	Maintenance (year 15)	Thinning 3: cleaning	1		3	23,873											23,873	42.8
15	Maintenance (year 15)	Annual fixed costs	1			36,188						Telephone, Electricity		per year	10,000	10,000	46,188	82.9
		SUBTOTAL:															**78,019**	**140.0**
t	Maintenance (year t)	Mowing	1	6.5	6.5	51,725											51,725	92.8
t	Maintenance (year t)	Round firewalls	1	4	4	31,831											31,831	57.1
t	Maintenance (year t)	Annual fixed costs	1			36,188						Telephone, Electricity		per year	10,000	10,000	46,188	82.9
		SUBTOTAL:															**129,744**	**232.8**
T	Maintenance (year T)	Visits forestry technicians	2									Visit		per visit	12,000	24,000	24,000	43.1
T	Maintenance (year T)	Annual fixed costs	1			36,188						Telephone, Electricity		per year	10,000	10,000	46,188	82.9
		SUBTOTAL:															**70,188**	**125.9**

Source: own elaborations based on consultations and CATIE (2005)

Appendix C

Regression analysis results of Stata

Sequential multiple regression model

```
. reg  lg_vol_tot inv_tree_age sqrt_precip_total temp_max_ma

      Source |       SS       df       MS              Number of obs =     599
-------------+------------------------------           F(  3,   595) =  518.81
       Model | 383.537966      3  127.845989           Prob > F      =  0.0000
    Residual | 146.619867    595  .246419945           R-squared     =  0.7234
-------------+------------------------------           Adj R-squared =  0.7220
       Total | 530.157833    598   .88655156           Root MSE      = .49641


  lg_vol_tot |    Coef.   Std. Err.      t    P>|t|     [95% Conf. Interval]
-------------+----------------------------------------------------------------
inv_tree_age |  -8.641259   .2391868   -36.13   0.000    -9.111012   -8.171506
 sqrt_preci~l |   .0202537   .0034474     5.88   0.000     .0134832    .0270242
 temp_max_ma | -.1845761   .0266005    -6.94   0.000    -.2368185   -.1323337
       _cons |  4.790801   .9265083     5.17   0.000     2.971177    6.610426
```

Stepwise regression model

```
reg  lg_vol_tot inv_tree_age  sqrt_precip_dry  temp_max_ma

      Source |       SS       df       MS              Number of obs =     599
-------------+------------------------------           F(  3,   595) =  508.38
       Model | 381.374094      3  127.124698           Prob > F      =  0.0000
    Residual | 148.783739    595  .250056704           R-squared     =  0.7194
-------------+------------------------------           Adj R-squared =  0.7179
       Total | 530.157833    598   .88655156           Root MSE      = .50006


  lg_vol_tot |    Coef.   Std. Err.      t    P>|t|     [95% Conf. Interval]
-------------+----------------------------------------------------------------
inv_tree_age |  -8.774858   .2394998   -36.64   0.000    -9.245226    -8.30449
 sqrt_preci~y |    .019724   .0039166     5.04   0.000     .012032    .0274159
 temp_max_ma | -.1970296   .0264687    -7.44   0.000    -.2490129   -.1450462
       _cons |  5.939672    .875478     6.78   0.000     4.220269    7.659075
```

Sequential multiple regression model with deleted outliers

```
reg  lg_vol_tot  inv_tree_age  sqrt_precip_total  temp_max_ma
```

```
      Source |       SS       df       MS              Number of obs =     592
-------------+------------------------------           F(  3,    588) =  749.09
       Model |  327.539759      3   109.17992           Prob > F      =  0.0000
    Residual |  85.7009566    588  .145749926           R-squared     =  0.7926
-------------+------------------------------           Adj R-squared =  0.7916
       Total |  413.240716    591  .69922287            Root MSE      =  .38177
```

```
------------------------------------------------------------------------------
  lg_vol_tot |     Coef.   Std. Err.      t    P>|t|     [95% Conf. Interval]
-------------+----------------------------------------------------------------
inv_tree_age |   -10.4583   .2427424   -43.08   0.000    -10.93505   -9.981553
 sqrt_preci~1 |   .0162734   .0026688     6.10   0.000      .011032    .0215149
  temp_max_ma |  -.1695049   .0205006    -8.27   0.000    -.2097682   -.1292415
        _cons |   4.675292   .7130173     6.56   0.000     3.274921    6.075663
------------------------------------------------------------------------------
```

Robust sequential multiple regression model

```
reg  lg_vol_tot  inv_tree_age  sqrt_precip_total  temp_max_ma, robust
```

```
Linear regression                                      Number of obs =     592
                                                       F(  3,    588) =  427.93
                                                       Prob > F      =  0.0000
                                                       R-squared     =  0.7926
                                                       Root MSE      =  .38177
```

```
------------------------------------------------------------------------------
             |              Robust
  lg_vol_tot |     Coef.   Std. Err.      t    P>|t|     [95% Conf. Interval]
-------------+----------------------------------------------------------------
inv_tree_age |   -10.4583   .3406359   -30.70   0.000    -11.12731   -9.789289
 sqrt_preci~1 |   .0162734   .0029253     5.56   0.000     .0105281    .0220187
  temp_max_ma |  -.1695049   .0272269    -6.23   0.000    -.2229787    -.116031
        _cons |   4.675292   .9600939     4.87   0.000     2.789661    6.560923
------------------------------------------------------------------------------
```

Appendix D

Average total tree volume per age of the tree data sample

Tree age	# of observations	Mean total volume (in m3)	Standard deviation	Min	Max
1	4	0.0038	0.0011	0.0026	0.0053
2	9	0.0106	0.0058	0.0027	0.0203
3	9	0.0286	0.0149	0.0078	0.0553
4	35	0.0863	0.0387	0.0020	0.1791
5	42	0.1101	0.0430	0.0044	0.2207
6	42	0.1434	0.0512	0.0080	0.2529
7	53	0.1724	0.0584	0.0140	0.3105
8	53	0.2097	0.0729	0.0207	0.3844
9	33	0.2236	0.0850	0.0304	0.4323
10	48	0.2741	0.0867	0.0505	0.4919
11	11	0.2932	0.1102	0.0726	0.5211
12	53	0.3157	0.0981	0.1046	0.5431
13	33	0.3273	0.0993	0.1551	0.6057
14	53	0.3815	0.1083	0.1857	0.7263
15	30	0.4030	0.1134	0.1946	0.8248
16	30	0.4326	0.1210	0.2078	0.8920
17	30	0.4648	0.1361	0.2208	1.0131
18	19	0.5145	0.1723	0.3336	1.1133
19	29	0.5250	0.1602	0.3492	1.2113
20	13	0.6092	0.2325	0.3775	1.2662
21	22	0.5930	0.1047	0.4015	0.7641
22	17	0.6576	0.1076	0.4644	0.8076
23	7	0.7896	0.0306	0.7275	0.8430
24	11	0.7358	0.1544	0.5011	0.8875
25	7	0.8936	0.0456	0.8119	0.9474
26	7	0.9375	0.0486	0.8378	0.9802
27	7	0.9996	0.0695	0.8611	1.0622
28	7	1.0610	0.0930	0.8838	1.1512
29	7	1.1353	0.1185	0.9293	1.3095
30	7	1.2302	0.1575	0.9580	1.4877
31	7	1.3077	0.1806	0.9899	1.5792
32	7	1.3891	0.2178	1.0115	1.7242
33	7	1.4665	0.2365	1.0360	1.8005
34	7	1.5494	0.2652	1.0585	1.9164
35	7	1.6218	0.2864	1.0885	1.9900
36	7	1.6775	0.3042	1.1111	2.0464
37	7	1.7291	0.2986	1.1390	2.0014
38	6	1.7402	0.3173	1.1707	2.0421
39	5	1.8186	0.3818	1.1971	2.1695
40	2	1.6381	0.6585	1.1725	2.1037

Source: own elaborations based on INISEFOR (without year a, without year b)

Appendix E

Volume scenarios in terms of merchantable timber and net CO_2e per tree age for historic and future climate conditions

VS	Tree age	Mean total volume (in m3/tree)	Mean commercial volume (in m3/tree)	Mean commercial volume (in m3/ha)	Total soil and biomass CO2e (in t/ha)	Total accumlated CO2e soil and biomass (in t/ha)	Total CO2e released at harvest (in t/ha)	Net CO2e (in t/ha)
Benchmark	0	0.00	0.00	0.00	825.00	0.00	0.00	0.00
	1	0.00	0.00	1.87	827.72	2.72	-2.06	0.66
	2	0.01	0.01	7.65	836.17	11.17	-8.46	2.71
	3	0.03	0.03	25.56	862.31	37.31	-28.26	9.05
	4	0.09	0.08	78.91	940.18	115.18	-87.24	27.94
	5	0.11	0.10	102.18	914.49	89.49	-112.97	-23.48
	6	0.14	0.13	80.38	942.34	117.34	-88.88	28.46
	7	0.17	0.16	96.97	966.54	141.54	-107.21	34.33
	8	0.21	0.20	118.23	997.58	172.58	-130.72	41.86
	9	0.22	0.21	126.13	1009.12	184.12	-139.46	44.66
	10	0.27	0.26	154.91	938.06	113.06	-171.27	-58.21
	11	0.29	0.28	82.92	946.04	121.04	-91.68	29.36
	12	0.32	0.30	89.28	955.33	130.33	-98.71	31.61
	13	0.33	0.31	92.57	960.13	135.13	-102.35	32.78
	14	0.38	0.36	108.02	982.68	157.68	-119.43	38.25
	15	0.40	0.38	114.13	908.30	83.30	-126.18	-42.89
	16	0.43	0.41	61.28	914.45	89.45	-67.75	21.70
	17	0.46	0.44	65.86	921.14	96.14	-72.82	23.32
	18	0.51	0.49	72.94	931.47	106.47	-80.64	25.82
	19	0.53	0.50	74.43	933.65	108.65	-82.29	26.35
	20	0.61	0.58	86.39	951.11	126.11	-95.52	30.59
	21	0.59	0.56	84.12	947.78	122.78	-93.00	29.78
	22	0.66	0.62	93.31	961.20	136.20	-103.16	33.04
	23	0.79	0.75	112.12	988.66	163.66	-123.96	39.70
	24	0.74	0.70	104.44	977.45	152.45	-115.47	36.98
	25	0.89	0.85	126.90	1010.24	185.24	-140.31	44.93
	26	0.94	0.89	133.16	1019.37	194.37	-147.22	47.15
	27	1.00	0.95	142.00	1032.28	207.28	-157.00	50.28
	28	1.06	1.00	150.73	1045.03	220.03	-166.66	53.37
	29	1.14	1.08	161.31	1060.46	235.46	-178.35	57.11
	30	1.23	1.17	174.81	1080.17	255.17	-193.28	61.89
	31	1.31	1.24	185.83	1096.26	271.26	-205.46	65.80
	32	1.39	1.32	197.42	1113.18	288.18	-218.28	69.90
	33	1.47	1.39	208.43	1129.25	304.25	-230.45	73.80
	34	1.55	1.47	220.21	1146.45	321.45	-243.48	77.97
	35	1.62	1.54	230.52	1161.50	336.50	-254.88	81.62
	36	1.68	1.59	238.44	1173.05	348.05	-263.63	84.42
	37	1.73	1.64	245.79	1183.79	358.79	-271.76	87.03
	38	1.74	1.65	247.37	1186.09	361.09	-273.50	87.59
	39	1.82	1.72	258.53	1202.37	377.37	-285.84	91.54
	40	1.64	1.55	232.84	1164.88	339.88	-257.44	82.44

Volume scenarios (continued)

VS	Tree age	Mean total volume (in m3/tree)	Mean commercial volume (in m3/tree)	Mean commercial volume (in m3/ha)	Total soil and biomass CO2e (in t/ha)	Total accumlated CO2e soil and biomass (in t/ha)	Total CO2e released at harvest (in t/ha)	Net CO2e (in t/ha)
VS_PRECIS_1	0	0.00	0.00	0.00	825.00	0.00	0.00	0.00
	1	0.00	0.00	0.63	825.92	0.92	-0.69	0.22
	2	0.00	0.00	2.58	828.76	3.76	-2.85	0.91
	3	0.01	0.01	8.60	837.56	12.56	-9.51	3.05
	4	0.03	0.03	26.56	863.76	38.76	-29.36	9.40
	5	0.04	0.03	34.39	855.12	30.12	-38.02	-7.90
	6	0.05	0.05	27.05	864.49	39.49	-29.91	9.58
	7	0.06	0.05	32.63	872.63	47.63	-36.08	11.55
	8	0.07	0.07	39.79	883.08	58.08	-43.99	14.09
	9	0.08	0.07	42.45	886.96	61.96	-46.93	15.03
	10	0.09	0.09	52.13	863.05	38.05	-57.64	-19.59
	11	0.10	0.09	27.91	865.73	40.73	-30.85	9.88
	12	0.11	0.10	30.05	868.86	43.86	-33.22	10.64
	13	0.11	0.10	31.15	870.48	45.48	-34.45	11.03
	14	0.13	0.12	36.35	878.06	53.06	-40.19	12.87
	15	0.14	0.13	38.41	853.03	28.03	-42.47	-14.43
	16	0.15	0.14	20.62	855.10	30.10	-22.80	7.30
	17	0.16	0.15	22.16	857.35	32.35	-24.51	7.85
	18	0.17	0.16	24.55	860.83	35.83	-27.14	8.69
	19	0.18	0.17	25.05	861.56	36.56	-27.70	8.87
	20	0.21	0.19	29.07	867.44	42.44	-32.15	10.29
	21	0.20	0.19	28.31	866.32	41.32	-31.30	10.02
	22	0.22	0.21	31.40	870.84	45.84	-34.72	11.12
	23	0.27	0.25	37.73	880.08	55.08	-41.72	13.36
	24	0.25	0.23	35.15	876.30	51.30	-38.86	12.44
	25	0.30	0.28	42.71	887.34	62.34	-47.22	15.12
	26	0.32	0.30	44.81	890.41	65.41	-49.55	15.87
	27	0.34	0.32	47.79	894.76	69.76	-52.84	16.92
	28	0.36	0.34	50.73	899.05	74.05	-56.09	17.96
	29	0.38	0.36	54.29	904.24	79.24	-60.02	19.22
	30	0.41	0.39	58.83	910.88	85.88	-65.05	20.83
	31	0.44	0.42	62.54	916.29	91.29	-69.15	22.14
	32	0.47	0.44	66.44	921.98	96.98	-73.46	23.52
	33	0.49	0.47	70.15	927.39	102.39	-77.56	24.84
	34	0.52	0.49	74.11	933.18	108.18	-81.94	26.24
	35	0.55	0.52	77.58	938.25	113.25	-85.78	27.47
	36	0.56	0.53	80.25	942.13	117.13	-88.72	28.41
	37	0.58	0.55	82.72	945.75	120.75	-91.46	29.29
	38	0.59	0.56	83.25	946.52	121.52	-92.04	29.48
	39	0.61	0.58	87.00	952.00	127.00	-96.20	30.81
	40	0.55	0.52	78.36	939.38	114.38	-86.64	27.74

Volume scenarios (continued)

VS	Tree age	Mean total volume (in m3/tree)	Mean commercial volume (in m3/tree)	Mean commercial volume (in m3/ha)	Total soil and biomass CO2e (in t/ha)	Total accumlated CO2e soil and biomass (in t/ha)	Total CO2e released at harvest (in t/ha)	Net CO2e (in t/ha)
VS_PRECIS_2	0	0.00	0.00	0.00	825.00	0.00	0.00	0.00
	1	0.00	0.00	1.54	827.24	2.24	-1.70	0.54
	2	0.01	0.01	6.30	834.20	9.20	-6.97	2.23
	3	0.02	0.02	21.04	855.71	30.71	-23.26	7.45
	4	0.07	0.06	64.96	919.82	94.82	-71.82	23.00
	5	0.09	0.08	84.12	898.67	73.67	-93.00	-19.33
	6	0.12	0.11	66.17	921.60	96.60	-73.17	23.43
	7	0.14	0.13	79.83	941.52	116.52	-88.26	28.26
	8	0.17	0.16	97.33	967.07	142.07	-107.61	34.46
	9	0.18	0.17	103.84	976.57	151.57	-114.81	36.76
	10	0.23	0.21	127.53	918.08	93.08	-141.00	-47.92
	11	0.24	0.23	68.26	924.64	99.64	-75.47	24.17
	12	0.26	0.25	73.50	932.29	107.29	-81.27	26.02
	13	0.27	0.25	76.21	936.24	111.24	-84.26	26.98
	14	0.31	0.30	88.92	954.80	129.80	-98.32	31.49
	15	0.33	0.31	93.95	893.57	68.57	-103.88	-35.31
	16	0.36	0.34	50.45	898.64	73.64	-55.78	17.86
	17	0.38	0.36	54.22	904.14	79.14	-59.95	19.20
	18	0.42	0.40	60.04	912.65	87.65	-66.39	21.26
	19	0.43	0.41	61.27	914.44	89.44	-67.75	21.69
	20	0.50	0.47	71.12	928.82	103.82	-78.63	25.18
	21	0.49	0.46	69.25	926.08	101.08	-76.56	24.52
	22	0.54	0.51	76.81	937.12	112.12	-84.93	27.20
	23	0.65	0.62	92.30	959.73	134.73	-102.05	32.68
	24	0.61	0.57	85.98	950.50	125.50	-95.06	30.44
	25	0.74	0.70	104.47	977.50	152.50	-115.51	36.99
	26	0.77	0.73	109.62	985.01	160.01	-121.20	38.81
	27	0.82	0.78	116.90	995.64	170.64	-129.25	41.39
	28	0.87	0.83	124.09	1006.13	181.13	-137.20	43.94
	29	0.93	0.89	132.79	1018.84	193.84	-146.82	47.02
	30	1.01	0.96	143.91	1035.07	210.07	-159.11	50.95
	31	1.08	1.02	152.98	1048.31	223.31	-169.14	54.17
	32	1.14	1.08	162.52	1062.24	237.24	-179.69	57.54
	33	1.21	1.14	171.59	1075.47	250.47	-189.71	60.75
	34	1.28	1.21	181.29	1089.62	264.62	-200.44	64.19
	35	1.34	1.27	189.78	1102.02	277.02	-209.82	67.19
	36	1.38	1.31	196.29	1111.53	286.53	-217.03	69.50
	37	1.42	1.35	202.35	1120.37	295.37	-223.72	71.64
	38	1.43	1.36	203.64	1122.26	297.26	-225.16	72.10
	39	1.50	1.42	212.83	1135.67	310.67	-235.31	75.35
	40	1.35	1.28	191.68	1104.80	279.80	-211.93	67.87

Volume scenarios (continued)

VS	Tree age	Mean total volume (in m3/tree)	Mean commercial volume (in m3/tree)	Mean commercial volume (in m3/ha)	Total soil and biomass CO2e (in t/ha)	Total accumulated CO2e soil and biomass (in t/ha)	Total CO2e released at harvest (in t/ha)	Net CO2e (in t/ha)
	0	0.00	0.00	0.00	825.00	0.00	0.00	0.00
	1	0.00	0.00	0.89	826.30	1.30	-0.99	0.32
	2	0.01	0.00	3.66	830.34	5.34	-4.05	1.30
	3	0.01	0.01	12.23	842.85	17.85	-13.52	4.33
	4	0.04	0.04	37.75	880.10	55.10	-41.74	13.37
	5	0.05	0.05	48.88	867.81	42.81	-54.05	-11.23
	6	0.07	0.06	38.46	881.13	56.13	-42.52	13.62
	7	0.08	0.08	46.39	892.71	67.71	-51.29	16.42
	8	0.10	0.09	56.56	907.56	82.56	-62.53	20.03
	9	0.11	0.10	60.34	913.08	88.08	-66.72	21.36
	10	0.13	0.12	74.11	879.09	54.09	-81.94	-27.85
	11	0.14	0.13	39.67	882.90	57.90	-43.86	14.05
	12	0.15	0.14	42.71	887.35	62.35	-47.22	15.12
	13	0.16	0.15	44.29	889.64	64.64	-48.96	15.68
	14	0.18	0.17	51.68	900.43	75.43	-57.13	18.30
	15	0.19	0.18	54.60	864.85	39.85	-60.36	-20.52
	16	0.21	0.20	29.32	867.79	42.79	-32.41	10.38
	17	0.22	0.21	31.51	870.99	45.99	-34.84	11.16
	18	0.25	0.23	34.89	875.93	50.93	-38.58	12.35
VS_MMD_1	19	0.25	0.24	35.61	876.98	51.98	-39.37	12.61
	20	0.29	0.28	41.33	885.33	60.33	-45.70	14.63
	21	0.28	0.27	40.24	883.74	58.74	-44.49	14.25
	22	0.31	0.30	44.64	890.16	65.16	-49.35	15.80
	23	0.38	0.36	53.64	903.29	78.29	-59.30	18.99
	24	0.35	0.33	49.96	897.93	72.93	-55.24	17.69
	25	0.43	0.40	60.71	913.62	88.62	-67.12	21.50
	26	0.45	0.42	63.70	917.98	92.98	-70.43	22.55
	27	0.48	0.45	67.93	924.16	99.16	-75.11	24.05
	28	0.51	0.48	72.11	930.26	105.26	-79.73	25.53
	29	0.54	0.51	77.17	937.64	112.64	-85.32	27.32
	30	0.59	0.56	83.63	947.07	122.07	-92.46	29.61
	31	0.63	0.59	88.90	954.77	129.77	-98.29	31.48
	32	0.66	0.63	94.44	962.86	137.86	-104.42	33.44
	33	0.70	0.66	99.71	970.55	145.55	-110.25	35.30
	34	0.74	0.70	105.35	978.78	153.78	-116.48	37.30
	35	0.78	0.74	110.28	985.98	160.98	-121.93	39.05
	36	0.80	0.76	114.07	991.51	166.51	-126.12	40.39
	37	0.83	0.78	117.59	996.64	171.64	-130.01	41.63
	38	0.83	0.79	118.34	997.74	172.74	-130.84	41.90
	39	0.87	0.82	123.68	1005.53	180.53	-136.74	43.79
	40	0.78	0.74	111.39	987.59	162.59	-123.16	39.44

Volume scenarios (continued)

VS	Tree age	Mean total volume (in m3/tree)	Mean commercial volume (in m3/tree)	Mean commercial volume (in m3/ha)	Total soil and biomass CO2e (in t/ha)	Total accumlated CO2e soil and biomass (in t/ha)	Total CO2e released at harvest (in t/ha)	Net CO2e (in t/ha)
VS_MMD_2	0	0.00	0.00	0.00	825.00	0.00	0.00	0.00
	1	0.00	0.00	1.49	827.17	2.17	-1.65	0.53
	2	0.01	0.01	6.10	833.91	8.91	-6.75	2.16
	3	0.02	0.02	20.38	854.76	29.76	-22.54	7.22
	4	0.07	0.06	62.94	916.87	91.87	-69.59	22.28
	5	0.09	0.08	81.50	896.38	71.38	-90.11	-18.73
	6	0.11	0.11	64.12	918.59	93.59	-70.89	22.70
	7	0.14	0.13	77.34	937.90	112.90	-85.51	27.38
	8	0.17	0.16	94.30	962.65	137.65	-104.26	33.39
	9	0.18	0.17	100.61	971.85	146.85	-111.23	35.62
	10	0.22	0.21	123.56	915.18	90.18	-136.61	-46.43
	11	0.23	0.22	66.14	921.54	96.54	-73.13	23.42
	12	0.25	0.24	71.21	928.95	103.95	-78.74	25.21
	13	0.26	0.25	73.84	932.78	107.78	-81.64	26.14
	14	0.30	0.29	86.16	950.76	125.76	-95.26	30.51
	15	0.32	0.30	91.03	891.44	66.44	-100.64	-34.21
	16	0.35	0.33	48.88	896.35	71.35	-54.04	17.31
	17	0.37	0.35	52.53	901.68	76.68	-58.08	18.60
	18	0.41	0.39	58.18	909.92	84.92	-64.32	20.60
	19	0.42	0.40	59.37	911.66	86.66	-65.64	21.02
	20	0.49	0.46	68.91	925.59	100.59	-76.19	24.40
	21	0.47	0.45	67.09	922.93	97.93	-74.18	23.75
	22	0.52	0.50	74.42	933.63	108.63	-82.28	26.35
	23	0.63	0.60	89.43	955.54	130.54	-98.87	31.66
	24	0.59	0.56	83.30	946.59	121.59	-92.10	29.49
	25	0.71	0.67	101.22	972.75	147.75	-111.91	35.84
	26	0.75	0.71	106.21	980.03	155.03	-117.43	37.60
	27	0.80	0.76	113.26	990.33	165.33	-125.23	40.10
	28	0.85	0.80	120.23	1000.50	175.50	-132.93	42.57
	29	0.91	0.86	128.66	1012.81	187.81	-142.25	45.55
	30	0.98	0.93	139.43	1028.53	203.53	-154.16	49.37
	31	1.04	0.99	148.22	1041.36	216.36	-163.88	52.48
	32	1.11	1.05	157.47	1054.85	229.85	-174.10	55.75
	33	1.17	1.11	166.25	1067.67	242.67	-183.81	58.86
	34	1.24	1.17	175.64	1081.39	256.39	-194.20	62.19
	35	1.29	1.23	183.87	1093.40	268.40	-203.29	65.10
	36	1.34	1.27	190.18	1102.61	277.61	-210.28	67.34
	37	1.38	1.31	196.05	1111.18	286.18	-216.76	69.41
	38	1.39	1.32	197.31	1113.01	288.01	-218.15	69.86
	39	1.45	1.37	206.20	1126.00	301.00	-227.99	73.01
	40	1.31	1.24	185.72	1096.09	271.09	-205.34	65.76

Source: own elaborations

143

Appendix F

Cost- benefit structure of 1 ha including timber benefits and PES for a rotation period of 40 years

Age (t)	Annual costs (col/ha)	Harvest costs (col/ha)	Timber benefits (col/ha)	PES	Annual net revenue (col/ha)
0	-425,106	0	0	227,399	-197,707
1	-428,164	0	0	90,960	-337,204
2	-462,198	0	0	68,220	-393,979
3	-421,432	0	0	45,480	-375,952
4	-348,834	0	0	22,740	-326,094
5	-118,061	-929,836	0	0	-1,047,897
6	-129,744	0	0	0	-129,744
7	-129,744	0	0	0	-129,744
8	-129,744	0	0	0	-129,744
9	-129,744	0	0	0	-129,744
10	-121,786	-1,762,095	73,129	0	-1,810,752
11	-129,744	0	0	0	-129,744
12	-129,744	0	0	0	-129,744
13	-129,744	0	0	0	-129,744
14	-129,744	0	0	0	-129,744
15	-78,019	-1,298,179	91,920	0	-1,284,278
16	-129,744	0	0	0	-129,744
17	-129,744	0	0	0	-129,744
18	-129,744	0	0	0	-129,744
19	-129,744	0	0	0	-129,744
20	-129,744	0	0	0	-129,744
21	-129,744	0	0	0	-129,744
22	-129,744	0	0	0	-129,744
23	-129,744	0	0	0	-129,744
24	-129,744	0	0	0	-129,744
25	-129,744	0	0	0	-129,744
26	-129,744	0	0	0	-129,744
27	-129,744	0	0	0	-129,744
28	-129,744	0	0	0	-129,744
29	-129,744	0	0	0	-129,744
30	-129,744	0	0	0	-129,744
31	-129,744	0	0	0	-129,744
32	-129,744	0	0	0	-129,744
33	-129,744	0	0	0	-129,744
34	-129,744	0	0	0	-129,744
35	-129,744	0	0	0	-129,744
36	-129,744	0	0	0	-129,744
37	-129,744	0	0	0	-129,744
38	-129,744	0	0	0	-129,744
39	-129,744	0	0	0	-129,744
40	-129,744	0	0	0	-129,744

Source: own elaborations

Appendix G

Illustration of the LEV, analysis considering timber and carbon sequestration benefits, and PFS

	Cash flow					Discounted cash flow															
Age (t)	Annual costs (col/ha)	Harvest costs (col/ha)	Timber benefits (col/ha)	PFS	Annual net revenue (col/ha)	0	1	2	3	4	5	6	7	8	9	10	11	12	13	14	15
0	-475,106	0	0	227,399	-197,707	-197,707	-206,126	-214,904	-224,055	-233,596	-243,545	-253,914	-264,727	-276,000	-287,753	-300,007	-312,782	-326,102	-339,988	-354,466	-369,561
1	-428,164	0	0	90,960	-337,204		-337,204	-351,563	-366,534	-382,143	-398,416	-415,382	-433,070	-451,522	-470,739	-490,785	-511,684	-533,474	-556,191	-579,876	-604,569
2	-462,198	0	0	68,220	-393,979			-393,979	-410,756	-428,247	-446,484	-465,497	-485,319	-505,986	-527,533	-549,997	-573,416	-597,836	-623,294	-649,817	-677,509
3	-421,412	0	0	45,480	-375,932				-375,932	-391,961	-408,653	-426,054	-444,187	-463,113	-482,834	-503,385	-524,832	-547,181	-570,482	-594,775	-620,103
4	-398,834	0	0	22,740	-376,094					-376,094	-391,961	-408,653	-426,054	-444,187	-463,113	-482,834	-503,385	-524,832	-547,181	-570,482	-594,775
5	-1,138,061	-929,836	0	0	-1,047,897						-1,047,897	-1,092,520	-1,139,044	-1,187,548	-1,238,179	-1,290,842	-1,345,811	-1,403,121	-1,462,871	-1,525,186	-1,590,113
6	-129,744	0	0	0	-129,744							-129,744	-135,269	-141,029	-147,034	-153,296	-159,824	-166,629	-173,725	-181,123	-188,836
7	-129,744	0	0	0	-129,744								-129,744	-135,269	-141,029	-147,034	-153,296	-159,824	-166,629	-173,725	-181,123
8	-129,744	0	0	0	-129,744									-129,744	-135,269	-141,029	-147,034	-153,296	-159,824	-166,629	-173,725
9	-129,744	0	6,041,469	0	-129,744										-129,744	-135,269	-141,029	-147,034	-153,296	-159,824	-166,629
10	-121,786	-1,762,095	0	0	4,157,588											4,157,588	4,334,634	4,519,219	4,711,664	4,912,305	5,121,489
11	-129,744	0	0	0	-129,744												-129,744	-135,269	-141,029	-147,034	-153,296
12	-129,744	0	0	0	-129,744													-129,744	-135,269	-141,029	-147,034
13	-129,744	0	0	0	-129,744														-129,744	-135,269	-141,029
14	-129,744	0	0	0	-129,744															-129,744	-135,269
15	-78,019	-1,298,179	5,563,826	0	4,187,428																4,187,428
16	-129,744	0	0	0	-129,744																
17	-129,744	0	0	0	-129,744																
18	-129,744	0	0	0	-129,744																
19	-129,744	0	0	0	-129,744																
20	-129,744	0	0	0	-129,744																
21	-129,744	0	0	0	-129,744																
22	-129,744	0	0	0	-129,744																
23	-129,744	0	0	0	-129,744																
24	-129,744	0	0	0	-129,744																
25	-129,744	0	0	0	-129,744																
26	-129,744	0	0	0	-129,744																
27	-129,744	0	0	0	-129,744																
28	-129,744	0	0	0	-129,744																
29	-129,744	0	0	0	-129,744																
30	-129,744	0	0	0	-129,744																
31	-129,744	0	0	0	-129,744																
32	-129,744	0	0	0	-129,744																
33	-129,744	0	0	0	-129,744																
34	-129,744	0	0	0	-129,744																
35	-129,744	0	0	0	-129,744																
36	-129,744	0	0	0	-129,744																
37	-129,744	0	0	0	-129,744																
38	-129,744	0	0	0	-129,744																
39	-129,744	0	0	0	-129,744																
40	-129,744	0	0	0	-129,744																

Total net revenues for capital

		0	1	2	3	4	5	6	7	8	9	10	11	12	13	14	15
Timber value																	
Wood volume (m3/ha)																	57
Total revenues for timber sales (in ¢/ha)								9,454,128	11,527,195	12,297,898	7,551,637	8,084,757	8,705,073	9,025,767	10,521,789	5,563,826	
Total harvest costs (in ¢/ha)								-2,205,963	2,680,679	2,869,510	1,762,095	1,886,443	2,031,184	2,106,012	2,457,417	1,298,179	
Annual net revenues of timber (in ¢/ha)								7,248,165	8,637,517	9,428,388	5,789,741	6,198,314	6,673,889	6,919,755	8,074,371	4,265,647	
Carbon value																	
Accumulated carbon uptake of biomass and soil (t CO2e)	0.0	2.7	11.2	37.3	115.2	89.5	127.6	141.5	172.6	184.1	113.1	121.0	130.3	135.1	157.7	83.3	
Total revenues for carbon uptake (in ¢/ha)	0	12,454	51,056	170,469	526,406	409,001	536,263	646,882	788,728	841,462	516,721	553,185	595,629	617,572	720,619	380,681	
Accumulated carbon released at harvest (t CO2e)	0.0	-2.1	-8.5	-28.3	87.2	113.0	88.9	107.2	130.7	135.5	91.7	91.7	98.7	102.4	119.4	125.2	
Total costs for carbon release (in ¢/ha)	0	-9,433	-38,672	-129,149	-398,722	-516,323	-406,186	-489,575	-597,415	-637,357	-419,025	-451,154	-467,774	-645,826	174,793	-576,687	
Annual net revenues of carbon (in ¢/ha)	0	3,021	12,384	41,355	127,685	107,322	130,076	156,907	191,313	204,104	134,180	144,475	148,798	140,798	274,793	-196,006	
Total annual net revenues (timber and carbon) (in ¢/ha)	-197,707	3,021	12,384	41,356	127,685	-597,322	130,076	7,405,072	9,028,830	9,632,493	5,923,921	6,318,385	7,068,553	7,060,553	8,349,164	4,069,641	
Net compounded value (in ¢/ha)	-197,707	-543,190	-602,446	-1,377,290	-1,781,042	-2,884,973	-3,127,569	-3,905,340	-3,675,490	-3,961,250	-37,513	-307,456	-375,993	-373,993	-621,018	3,644,723	
Net compounded value total annual net revenue for capital (in ¢/ha)	-197,707	-540,369	-590,061	-1,335,941	-1,614,357	-2,902,295	-3,007,494	4,004,150	5,353,340	5,670,243	5,550,824	6,235,036	6,587,245	6,694,260	7,728,146	7,713,065	
Results								11,803,270	13,518,392	12,450,239	10,777,617	10,205,312	10,136,487	9,301,986	9,746,822	8,674,056	
Max LEV (in ¢/ha)	13,518,292																
Optimal rotation (in years)	8																

Source: own elaborations

Illustration of the LEV, analysis considering timber and carbon sequestration benefits, and PES (continued)

Cash flow						Discounted cash flow (continued)														
Age (t)	Annual costs (col/ha)	Harvest costs (col/ha)	Timber benefits (col/ha)	PES	Annual net revenue (col/ha)	16	17	18	19	20	21	22	23	24	25	26	27	28	29	30
0	-425,106	0	0	227,399	**-197,707**	**-385,298**	**-401,706**	**-418,812**	**-436,646**	**-455,240**	**-474,626**	**-494,838**	**-515,910**	**-537,879**	**-560,784**	**-584,664**	**-609,561**	**-635,519**	**-662,582**	**-690,797**
1	-428,164	0	0	90,960	**-337,204**	-630,314	-657,155	-685,139	-714,315	-744,733	-776,447	-809,511	-843,983	-879,923	-917,393	-956,459	-997,189	-1,039,653	-1,083,925	-1,130,083
2	-462,198	0	0	68,220	**-393,979**	-706,360	-736,439	-767,800	-800,495	-834,584	-870,123	-907,176	-945,807	-986,083	-1,028,075	-1,071,854	-1,117,497	-1,165,085	-1,214,698	-1,266,425
3	-421,432	0	0	45,480	**-375,952**	-646,509	-674,040	-702,743	-732,669	-763,868	-796,397	-830,310	-865,668	-902,531	-940,965	-981,034	-1,022,810	-1,066,366	-1,111,775	-1,159,119
4	-348,834	0	0	22,740	**-326,094**	-537,867	-560,771	-584,651	-609,548	-635,504	-662,567	-690,781	-720,197	-750,866	-782,841	-816,177	-850,933	-887,169	-924,948	-964,335
5	-118,061	-929,836	0	0	**-1,047,897**	-1,657,826	-1,728,423	-1,802,025	-1,878,762	-1,958,767	-2,042,179	-2,129,142	-2,219,809	-2,314,337	-2,412,890	-2,515,640	-2,622,765	-2,734,453	-2,850,896	-2,972,298
6	-129,744	0	0	0	**-129,744**	-196,877	-205,261	-214,002	-223,115	-232,616	-242,521	-252,849	-263,616	-274,842	-286,546	-298,748	-311,470	-324,733	-338,562	-352,979
7	-129,744	0	0	0	**-129,744**	-188,836	-196,877	-205,261	-214,002	-223,115	-232,616	-242,521	-252,849	-263,616	-274,842	-286,546	-298,748	-311,470	-324,733	-338,562
8	-129,744	0	0	0	**-129,744**	-181,123	-188,836	-196,877	-205,261	-214,002	-223,115	-232,616	-242,521	-252,849	-263,616	-274,842	-286,546	-298,748	-311,470	-324,733
9	-129,744	0	0	0	**-129,744**	-173,725	-181,123	-188,836	-196,877	-205,261	-214,002	-223,115	-232,616	-242,521	-252,849	-263,616	-274,842	-286,546	-298,748	-311,470
10	-121,786	-1,762,095	6,041,469	0	**4,157,588**	5,339,581	5,566,961	5,804,023	6,051,180	6,308,862	6,577,517	6,857,612	7,149,635	7,454,093	7,771,517	8,102,457	8,447,490	8,807,216	9,182,260	9,573,275
11	-129,744	0	0	0	**-129,744**	-159,824	-166,629	-173,725	-181,123	-188,836	-196,877	-205,261	-214,002	-223,115	-232,616	-242,521	-252,849	-263,616	-274,842	-286,546
12	-129,744	0	0	0	**-129,744**	-153,296	-159,824	-166,629	-173,725	-181,123	-188,836	-196,877	-205,261	-214,002	-223,115	-232,616	-242,521	-252,849	-263,616	-274,842
13	-129,744	0	0	0	**-129,744**	-147,034	-153,296	-159,824	-166,629	-173,725	-181,123	-188,836	-196,877	-205,261	-214,002	-223,115	-232,616	-242,521	-252,849	-263,616
14	-129,744	0	0	0	**-129,744**	-141,029	-147,034	-153,296	-159,824	-166,629	-173,725	-181,123	-188,836	-196,877	-205,261	-214,002	-223,115	-232,616	-242,521	-252,849
15	-78,019	-1,298,179	5,563,626	0	**4,187,428**	4,365,745	4,551,654	4,745,481	4,947,561	5,158,247	5,377,905	5,606,916	5,845,680	6,094,611	6,354,142	6,624,725	6,906,831	7,200,950	7,507,593	7,827,295
16	-129,744	0	0	0	**-129,744**	-129,744	-135,269	-141,029	-147,034	-153,296	-159,824	-166,629	-173,725	-181,123	-188,836	-196,877	-205,261	-214,002	-223,115	-232,616
17	-129,744	0	0	0	**-129,744**		-129,744	-135,269	-141,029	-147,034	-153,296	-159,824	-166,629	-173,725	-181,123	-188,836	-196,877	-205,261	-214,002	-223,115
18	-129,744	0	0	0	**-129,744**			-129,744	-135,269	-141,029	-147,034	-153,296	-159,824	-166,629	-173,725	-181,123	-188,836	-196,877	-205,261	-214,002
19	-129,744	0	0	0	**-129,744**				-129,744	-135,269	-141,029	-147,034	-153,296	-159,824	-166,629	-173,725	-181,123	-188,836	-196,877	-205,261
20	-129,744	0	0	0	**-129,744**					-129,744	-135,269	-141,029	-147,034	-153,296	-159,824	-166,629	-173,725	-181,123	-188,836	-196,877
21	-129,744	0	0	0	**-129,744**						-129,744	-135,269	-141,029	-147,034	-153,296	-159,824	-166,629	-173,725	-181,123	-188,836
22	-129,744	0	0	0	**-129,744**							-129,744	-135,269	-141,029	-147,034	-153,296	-159,824	-166,629	-173,725	-181,123
23	-129,744	0	0	0	**-129,744**								-129,744	-135,269	-141,029	-147,034	-153,296	-159,824	-166,629	-173,725
24	-129,744	0	0	0	**-129,744**									-129,744	-135,269	-141,029	-147,034	-153,296	-159,824	-166,629
25	-129,744	0	0	0	**-129,744**										-129,744	-135,269	-141,029	-147,034	-153,296	-159,824
26	-129,744	0	0	0	**-129,744**											-129,744	-135,269	-141,029	-147,034	-153,296
27	-129,744	0	0	0	**-129,744**												-129,744	-135,269	-141,029	-147,034
28	-129,744	0	0	0	**-129,744**													-129,744	-135,269	-141,029
29	-129,744	0	0	0	**-129,744**														-129,744	-135,269
30	-129,744	0	0	0	**-129,744**															-129,744
31	-129,744	0	0	0	**-129,744**															
32	-129,744	0	0	0	**-129,744**															
33	-129,744	0	0	0	**-129,744**															
34	-129,744	0	0	0	**-129,744**															
35	-129,744	0	0	0	**-129,744**															
36	-129,744	0	0	0	**-129,744**															
37	-129,744	0	0	0	**-129,744**															
38	-129,744	0	0	0	**-129,744**															
39	-129,744	0	0	0	**-129,744**															
40	-129,744	0	0	0	**-129,744**															
Total net revenues for capital																				
Timber value																				
Wood volume (m^3/ha)						61	66	73	74	86	84	93	112	104	127	133	142	151	161	175
Total revenues for timber sales (in ¢/ha)						5,974,851	6,421,384	7,111,392	7,256,941	8,423,272	8,201,227	9,097,275	10,931,506	10,182,563	12,373,227	12,982,693	13,844,940	14,696,463	15,727,278	17,043,916
Total harvest costs (in ¢/ha)						-1,394,132	-1,498,323	-1,659,325	-1,693,286	-1,965,430	-1,913,620	-2,122,697	-2,550,685	-2,375,931	-2,887,086	-3,029,295	-3,230,486	-3,429,175	-3,669,698	-3,976,914
Annual net revenues of timber (in ¢/ha)						4,580,719	4,923,061	5,452,067	5,563,655	6,457,842	6,287,607	6,974,577	8,380,821	7,806,632	9,486,141	9,953,398	10,614,454	11,267,288	12,057,580	13,067,002
Carbon value																				
Accumulated carbon uptake of biomass and soil (t CO_2e)						89.5	96.1	106.5	108.6	126.1	122.8	136.2	163.7	152.4	185.2	194.4	207.3	220.0	235.5	255.2
Total revenues for carbon uptake (in ¢/ha)						408,819	439,372	486,584	496,543	576,348	561,154	622,465	747,969	696,724	846,616	888,318	947,316	1,005,580	1,076,111	1,166,200
Accumulated carbon release at harvest (t CO_2e)						-67.8	-72.8	-80.6	-82.3	-95.5	-93.0	-103.2	-124.0	-115.5	-140.3	-147.2	-157.0	-166.7	-178.3	-193.3
Total costs for carbon release (in ¢/ha)						-309,656	-332,798	-368,559	-376,102	-436,549	-425,041	-471,480	-566,542	-527,727	-641,262	-672,848	-717,535	-761,667	-815,090	-883,327
Annual net revenues of carbon (in ¢/ha)						99,163	106,574	118,026	120,441	139,798	136,113	150,985	181,427	168,997	205,355	215,470	229,780	243,913	261,021	282,873
Total annual net revenues (timber and carbon) (in ¢/ha)						4,679,882	5,029,635	5,570,093	5,684,096	6,597,640	6,423,720	7,125,562	8,562,248	7,975,628	9,691,496	10,168,867	10,844,234	11,511,201	12,318,600	13,349,875
Net compounded value (in ¢/ha)						3,669,665	3,696,189	3,723,843	3,752,675	3,782,734	3,814,074	3,846,748	3,880,813	3,916,329	3,953,358	3,991,963	4,032,212	4,074,175	4,117,925	4,163,538
Net comp value+ total annual net revenue for capital (in ¢/ha)						8,349,547	8,725,824	9,293,936	9,436,771	10,380,375	10,237,794	10,972,310	12,443,061	11,891,958	13,644,853	14,160,830	14,876,447	15,585,376	16,436,526	17,513,413
LEV (in ¢/ha)						8,799,780	8,456,693	8,310,420	7,808,312	7,968,947	7,309,282	7,300,829	7,731,165	6,911,563	7,430,050	7,235,146	7,141,296	7,038,034	6,990,299	7,022,089
RESULTS																				
Max. LEV (in ¢/ha)					**13,518,292**															
Optimal rotation (in years)					**8**															

Illustration of the LEV$_J$ analysis considering timber and carbon sequestration benefits, and PES (continued)

	Cash flow				Discounted cash flow (continued)									
Age (t)	Annual costs (col/ha)	Harvest costs (col/ha)	Timber benefits (col/ha)	PES	Annual net revenue (col/ha)	31	32	33	34	35	36	37	38	39	40
0	-425,106			227,399	-197,707	-720,214	-750,883	-782,858	-816,195	-850,952	-887,189	-924,969	-964,357	-1,005,423	-1,048,238
1	-428,164			90,960	-337,204	-1,178,206	-1,228,379	-1,280,688	-1,335,224	-1,392,683	-1,451,363	-1,513,158	-1,577,604	-1,644,784	-1,714,825
2	-462,198			68,220	-393,979	-1,320,354	-1,376,579	-1,435,199	-1,496,316	-1,560,034	-1,626,466	-1,695,727	-1,767,938	-1,843,223	-1,921,715
3	-421,432			45,480	-375,952	-1,208,479	-1,259,640	-1,313,503	-1,369,531	-1,427,851	-1,488,854	-1,552,046	-1,618,138	-1,687,045	-1,758,866
4	-348,834			22,740	-326,094	-1,005,400	-1,048,214	-1,092,851	-1,139,389	-1,187,908	-1,238,494	-1,291,233	-1,346,219	-1,403,546	-1,463,314
5	-119,061	929,836		0	-1,047,897	-3,698,869	-3,282,821	-3,368,412	-3,511,851	-3,661,399	-3,817,315	-3,979,871	-4,149,349	-4,326,044	-4,510,289
6	-129,744			0	-129,744	-368,010	-383,681	-400,020	-417,059	-434,814	-453,330	-472,635	-492,761	-513,745	-535,622
7	-129,744			0	-129,744	-352,979	-368,010	-383,681	-400,020	-417,059	-434,814	-453,330	-472,635	-492,761	-513,745
8	-129,744			0	-129,744	-338,562	-352,979	-368,010	-383,681	-400,020	-417,059	-434,814	-453,330	-472,635	-492,761
9	-129,744			0	-129,744	-324,733	-338,562	-352,979	-368,010	-383,681	-400,020	-417,059	-434,814	-453,330	-472,635
10	-121,786	-1,762,095	9,041,469	0	4,157,588	9,880,941	10,405,067	10,849,092	11,311,086	11,792,759	12,294,936	12,818,501	13,364,390	13,933,485	14,526,804
11	-129,744			0	-129,744	-298,748	-311,470	-324,733	-338,562	-352,979	-368,010	-383,681	-400,020	-417,059	-434,814
12	-129,744			0	-129,744	-286,546	-298,748	-311,470	-324,733	-338,562	-352,979	-368,010	-383,681	-400,020	-417,059
13	-129,744			0	-129,744	-274,833	-286,546	-298,748	-311,470	-324,733	-338,562	-352,979	-368,010	-383,681	-400,020
14	-129,744			0	-129,744	-263,616	-274,833	-286,546	-298,748	-311,470	-324,733	-338,562	-352,979	-368,010	-383,681
15	-78,019	5,563,626		0	4,187,628	8,160,610	8,508,120	8,870,427	9,248,164	9,641,985	10,052,577	10,480,654	10,926,959	11,392,270	11,877,396
16	-129,744			0	-129,744	-242,521	-252,849	-263,616	-274,842	-286,546	-298,748	-311,470	-324,733	-338,562	-352,979
17	-129,744			0	-129,744	-232,616	-242,521	-252,849	-263,616	-274,842	-286,546	-298,748	-311,470	-324,733	-338,562
18	-129,744			0	-129,744	-223,115	-232,616	-242,521	-252,849	-263,616	-274,842	-286,546	-298,748	-311,470	-324,733
19	-129,744			0	-129,744	-214,002	-223,115	-232,616	-242,521	-252,849	-263,616	-274,842	-286,546	-298,748	-311,470
20	-129,744			0	-129,744	-205,261	-214,002	-223,115	-232,616	-242,521	-252,849	-263,616	-274,842	-286,546	-298,748
21	-129,744			0	-129,744	-196,877	-205,261	-214,002	-223,115	-232,616	-242,521	-252,849	-263,616	-274,842	-286,546
22	-129,744			0	-129,744	-188,836	-196,877	-205,261	-214,002	-223,115	-232,616	-242,521	-252,849	-263,616	-274,842
23	-129,744			0	-129,744	-181,123	-188,836	-196,877	-205,261	-214,002	-223,115	-232,616	-242,521	-252,849	-263,616
24	-129,744			0	-129,744	-173,725	-181,123	-188,836	-196,877	-205,261	-214,002	-223,115	-232,616	-242,521	-252,849
25	-129,744			0	-129,744	-166,629	-173,725	-181,123	-188,836	-196,877	-205,261	-214,002	-223,115	-232,616	-242,521
26	-129,744			0	-129,744	-159,824	-166,629	-173,725	-181,123	-188,836	-196,877	-205,261	-214,002	-223,115	-232,616
27	-129,744			0	-129,744	-153,296	-159,824	-166,629	-173,725	-181,123	-188,836	-196,877	-205,261	-214,002	-223,115
28	-129,744			0	-129,744	-147,034	-153,296	-159,824	-166,629	-173,725	-181,123	-188,836	-196,877	-205,261	-214,002
29	-129,744			0	-129,744	-141,029	-147,034	-153,296	-159,824	-166,629	-173,725	-181,123	-188,836	-196,877	-205,261
30	-129,744			0	-129,744	-135,269	-141,029	-147,034	-153,296	-159,824	-166,629	-173,725	-181,123	-188,836	-196,877
31	-129,744			0	-129,744	-129,744	-135,269	-141,029	-147,034	-153,296	-159,824	-166,629	-173,725	-181,123	-188,836
32	-129,744			0	-129,744		-129,744	-135,269	-141,029	-147,034	-153,296	-159,824	-166,629	-173,725	-181,123
33	-129,744			0	-129,744			-129,744	-135,269	-141,029	-147,034	-153,296	-159,824	-166,629	-173,725
34	-129,744			0	-129,744				-129,744	-135,269	-141,029	-147,034	-153,296	-159,824	-166,629
35	-129,744			0	-129,744					-129,744	-135,269	-141,029	-147,034	-153,296	-159,824
36	-129,744			0	-129,744						-129,744	-135,269	-141,029	-147,034	-153,296
37	-129,744			0	-129,744							-129,744	-135,269	-141,029	-147,034
38	-129,744			0	-129,744								-129,744	-135,269	-141,029
39	-129,744			0	-129,744									-129,744	-135,269
40	-129,744			0	-129,744										-129,744

Total net revenues for capital		
		13,518,292
		8

Timber value

		31	32	33	34	35	36	37	38	39	40
Wood volume (m³/ha)		189	197	208	208	220	231	238	246	247	259	233
Total revenue for timber sales (in ₡/ha)		18,116,391	19,248,549	20,311,967	21,470,703	22,476,153	23,247,991	23,944,991	24,118,953	25,206,278	22,701,855
Total harvest costs (in ₡/ha)		-4,227,624	-4,491,328	-4,741,792	-5,009,631	-5,244,436	-5,474,531	-5,591,831	-5,627,662	-5,881,465	-5,297,099
Annual net revenue of timber (in ₡/ha)		13,890,766	14,757,221	15,580,175	16,460,872	17,231,717	17,823,460	18,373,160	18,490,390	18,325,813	17,404,755

Carbon value

		31	32	33	34	35	36	37	38	39	40
Accumulated carbon uptake of biomass and soil (t CO2e)		271.3	288.2	304.7	321.4	366.5	348.1	358.8	361.1	377.4	339.9
Total revenue for carbon uptake (in ₡/ha)		1,239,719	1,317,048	1,390,495	1,469,695	1,537,891	1,590,703	1,639,762	1,650,269	1,724,605	1,553,334
Accumulated carbon release at harvest (t CO2e)		-205.5	-218.3	-230.4	-243.5	-254.9	-263.6	-271.8	-273.5	-285.8	-257.4
Total costs for carbon release (in ₡/ha)		-939,013	-997,586	-1,063,217	-1,112,732	-1,164,861	-1,204,863	-1,242,023	-1,249,981	-1,306,354	-1,176,559
Annual net revenue of carbon (in ₡/ha)		300,705	319,543	337,343	356,963	373,030	385,840	397,740	400,388	418,142	376,776

		31	32	33	34	35	36	37	38	39	40
Total annual net revenue (timber and carbon) (in ₡/ha)		14,191,472	15,076,694	15,917,457	16,817,215	17,604,747	18,209,300	18,770,900	18,891,179	18,743,154	17,781,531
Net compounded value (in ₡/ha)		4,211,094	4,202,075	4,312,367	4,260,260	4,422,448	4,481,029	4,542,104	4,605,780	4,672,168	4,741,383
Net comp value total annual net revenue for capital (in ₡/ha)		18,402,566	19,337,358	20,229,319	21,183,474	22,027,195	22,690,328	23,313,004	23,496,958	24,415,322	22,522,914
LEV (in ₡/ha)		6,963,190	6,911,232	6,835,108	6,771,537	6,666,694	6,506,382	6,357,663	6,059,489	5,976,262	5,235,475

Max. LEV (in ₡/ha)	13,518,292
Optimal rotation (in years)	8

149

Appendix H

Personal communications

Hernández, Luis (a) (CACN):	Telephone consultation on 22-10-2008
Hernández, Luis (b) (CACN):	Telephone consultation on 18-09-2008
Hotel operator (Cabuya- Puntarenas):	Consultation on 04-10-2008
Meza, Victor H. (a) (INISEFOR):	Consultation on 08-09-2008
Meza, Victor H. (b) (INISEFOR):	E-mail consultation on 12-05-2009
Meza, Victor H. (c) (INISEFOR):	E-mail consultation on 13-05-2009
Retana, José A. (IMN):	Consultation on 01-10-2008
Sawmill staff member	
(Sawmill 'La Mansion', Nicoya):	Telephone consultation on 21-10-2008
Teak producer (Nandayure-Guanacaste):	Telephone interview on 18-10-2008

ibidem-Verlag

Melchiorstr. 15

D-70439 Stuttgart

info@ibidem-verlag.de

www.ibidem-verlag.de
www.ibidem.eu
www.edition-noema.de
www.autorenbetreuung.de